W9-BPP-901

3-2014

GERMAN AIRBORNE TROOPS

GERMAN AIRBORNE TROOPS 1936-45
Roger Edwards

DOUBLEDAY & COMPANY, INC.
Garden City, New York

Printed in Great Britain

Copyright © Roger Edwards 1974
First published in Great Britain in 1974 by
Macdonald and Jane's, London

ISBN 0-385-04246 9

Library of Congress Catalog Card Number 74-9156

Series Consultant Editor: Roger Edwards

Layout and make-up: Michael Jarvis

Contents

Foreword   7

1. Introduction and Acknowledgments   9
2. Uniform, Combat Dress and Battle Equipment   13
3. Weapons   27
4. Air Transport   37
5. Training and Organisation   51
6. Military Operations — Early Days   63
7. Military Operations — Airborne Assault   71
8. Military Operations — on Every Front   99
9. Unit Histories   135
10. Personalities   145

Foreword

When the future Field-Marshal Earl Wavell returned to Britain after witnessing the Soviet military manoeuvres in 1935, he displayed no real interest in the air-landing and parachute exercises conducted by the Soviet army and air force at Kiev. Consequently no one in Britain gave much thought before 1939 to the new and exciting concept of airborne warfare.

A small band of Germans, however, thought otherwise and we it was who developed this new weapon, often in the face of the ignorance and indifference of our own arch-conservative military establishment. Even so, in the early war years, German airborne forces achieved military success that caused the world to gasp. Chosen by fate, I was to lead our parachute forces. The German paratrooper's qualities of idealism, initiative and courage set up milestones along a harsh road that led through Dombas, Narvik, Eban-Emael, Fortress Holland, Corinth and Crete. Thereafter, the parachute troops served in the rôle of infantry, true to their soldierly reputation, whenever trouble occurred on any front, in Russia, North Africa, Sicily, Italy, France, Belgium and Holland.

The Allies, needless to say, made good use of early German experience and built up a powerful airborne army. The strategic objectives of our former opponents and the development of their airborne forces took the same direction as I had intended for the German *Fallschirmjäger.*

I see the mark of a true soldier in the author's presentation of this account of the growth of the German airborne idea from birth through military climax to premature death in Crete. This book also honours those who died in the war; reminded of their achievements as soldiers, we who still live benefit immeasurably by their example.

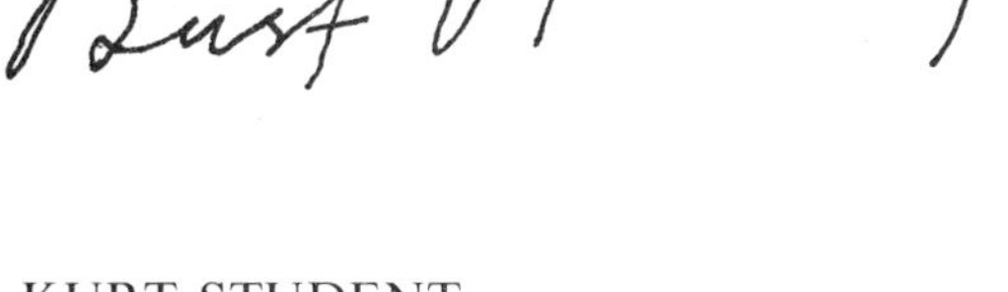

Kurt Student

KURT STUDENT
Generaloberst a.D.
former Commander of German Airborne Forces

7

The Reich Minister for Air Transport and
Supreme Commander of the Air Force

Berlin, 29th January 1936

S E C R E T

Air District II

The following order is for Regiment 'General Göring' to train
in parachute jumping.

On a basis of voluntary enrolment fifteen officers, junior
officers and junior leaders of the regiment are to be trained
as future instructors. Suitable volunteers should weigh
under 85 kilo (including clothing), be in good physical condi-
tion and be passed as medically fit for flying duties.

Commencement of training: provisionally set for 1st May 1936.

Period of training: eight weeks, out of which four weeks will
be devoted to training as parachute observer with the air
force equipment inspectorate, followed by four weeks of
practical training in parachute jumping from an aeroplane.
The airfield allotted to this purpose in Neubrandenburg.

A Ju 52 will be allocated by the Reich Air Ministry (LC). The
Reich Air Ministry (LA III) will provide suitable instructors.

LKK II is to confirm the following by 15th March 1936:

1. Name and rank of volunteers
2. Completion of medical examination for flying fitness
3. Suitability of designated airfield. If necessary, another
    suggestion is to be put forward.

Establishment costs are to be forwarded to Kap A 2 Tit. 24,
sub-section 4b, for special attention.

For the duration of the four week practical training in parachute jumping the pilot allowance DRdLLP 4010/35 1 1 A g v e
5 35, code LV b (Front Group), XX is authorised.

Signed

MILCH

1 Introduction

At first light on the morning of 10th May 1940 a detachment of German gliderborne troops, their existence until that moment a closely guarded secret, swept effortlessly on to Fort Eban-Emael, situated a few miles south of Maastricht on the Belgian frontier with Holland. Within minutes of their landing, fourteen medium and heavy calibre guns, the main armaments of the fortress, all mounted in armoured casemates, lay crippled or blasted into fragments by ingeniously devised demolition charges.

Until that time Eban-Emael protected by the steep and deeply cut Albert Canal, anti-tank walls and ditches and defended by more than a thousand well-trained troops, had been looked upon as impregnable by the Belgian general staff. Nevertheless, the fortress – the northern anchor in the Belgian frontier defences – fell to a force of fewer than sixty men in a precisely executed airborne attack that in the act left few hopes for the defence of Belgium.

Earlier, in April, German parachute troops had participated in surprise attacks on Denmark and Norway, assisting the passage of conventional land forces by the seizure of vital bridges and airfields. Denmark collapsed at once and Norway two months later. In similar fashion on 10th May in Holland, at Rotterdam, The Hague, Moerdijk and at Dordrecht, gliderborne and parachute troops of the German Luftwaffe paralysed the Dutch defensive systems.

Thanks to the brilliant action at Eban-Emael: the equally successful raids on nearby bridges and the airborne assault on 'Fortress Holland', two German Army Groups drove deeply from easterly and southerly directions into Belgium and Holland. Assisted also by devastating air raids on key cities, their progress was swift and losses slight. Further south more German armies were moving over the French frontier between the Oise and the Meuse south of Sedan; but the *coup de grâce*, delivered simultaneously with the isolation of Belgium and Holland was effected across the difficult terrain of the Ardennes Forest. Here von Runstedt's Army Group A brushed aside or bypassed all opposition and raced for the Channel ports. Within days the omnipotent Wehrmacht held much of Western Europe in its grasp, and the downfall of the French nation was near at hand.

German airborne troops later accompanied Twelfth Army into the Balkans in April 1941. In Greece on 26th April the airborne assault at Corinth and capture of the bridge all but succeeded in blocking the withdrawal of British forces to easterly Greek ports.

The culmination of the German Balkan operation came with the spectacular attack by the German 7th Air Division on the Mediterranean island of Crete. Here, commencing on 20th May, German airborne forces conclusively proved their worth in the strategic deployment of a modern army. In spite of stiff resistance from British, Dominion and Greek troops, the conquest of Crete was completed in little more than a week.

Sadly depleted in numbers after the Battle of Crete, the survivors of the Mediterranean adventure demonstrated sterling qualities in the arduous conditions that prevailed on the Russian front; highly trained, specialist troops being sacrificed in the traditional rôle of infantry.

Ultimately ten in number, German parachute divisions were to campaign in Libya, Tunisia, Italy, Russia, France, Belgium, Holland and in the German homeland. When the end was near at hand in the autumn of 1944, First Parachute Army stood astride the North West approaches to Germany in 'Fortress Holland' under the command of their creator, *Generaloberst* Kurt Student. Here where four years earlier a cold dawn had first hinted at their clandestine presence, the *Fallschirmjäger* faced Allied airborne forces patterned closely on the original German model. But, vitality drained by years of action, inadequately equipped and grounded for want of transport, the German airborne soldiers gave ground. Defending the Lower Rhineland in a resolute engagement near Nijmegen in the Reichswald on the German border, the paratroopers at last succumbed to the material superiority of Allied arms. The survivors of the once proud airborne battalions shared the ignominy of defeat in Allied prisoner-of-war camps with compatriots from worn-out and run-down Wehrmacht battalions; survivors also of the equally proud armoured, motorised and infantry divisions that once ranged the length and breadth of Europe.

The achievement of *Generaloberst* Student and the German airborne forces in pioneering the principles of vertical envelopment is reflected in the military establishments of today's great powers. The Warsaw Pact signatories maintain large, powerful airborne forces; and the armies of the Western alliance support airborne formations which are at least staffed effectively in relation to their respective strengths.

Clearly, the strategic deployment of troops by global transport has added a new dimension to the means of delivering troops by air into battle. New techniques of lifting troops into action by helicopter with the support of gunships have already been tested with success in Vietnam. Since the war new methods of rigging and lifting heavy equipment, artillery and stores by air and their delivery at the dropping zone, as well as improved techniques of resupply during the various phases of the battle, have largely superseded experimental war-time logistic schemes. The military application of free-fall parachuting raises new possibilities for dropping small parties of parachutists behind the enemy lines. But it is to the credit of the German airborne forces in the Second World War that they were the first to give practical expression to the military effectiveness of vertical envelopment and inaugurated traditions of airborne warfare to which modern armies of the world are heir.

Acknowledgments

Many people, and I am greatly indebted to them, have generously assisted with material for this study of German airborne forces.

Herr Oswald Finzel, a former battalion commander of *Fallschirmjäger Regiment* 6, contributed much of the biographical detail in Section 10 and placed at my disposal the archives of the *Fallschirmjäger Bund.* I am grateful to him.

Barry Gregory, formerly of the airborne RA, kindly read the manuscript and made many useful suggestions; Mary Field worked unceasingly to coordinate the British and German editorial contributions.

The photographs, unless otherwise stated, are from the *Bildarchiv* at Koblenz and were selected with the help of Dr Haupt. The maps were drawn by Robert Taylor. I wish to thank them all.

Berliner
Illustrierte Zeitung

Neun Tage lang abgeschnitten!

Deutsche Fallschirmjäger wurden bei Herakleion abgesetzt, ohne Verbindung mit den anderen auf Kreta operierenden Einheiten. In erbitterten Kämpfen schlugen sie sich neun Tage lang gegen eine gewaltige Übermacht. Nur tasten sie in einer verlassenen Stadt. Ein Kätzchen, weil sind auch das erste Lebewesen, gesellt sich zu ihnen. Zum großen Bildbericht im Inneren des Heftes.

PK. Bildbox 392

1941 magazine cover illustrating combat dress worn during the attack on Crete. Note the side-lacing boots and helmet cover. Caption refers to Herakleion where these men from Group East (FJR 1) were cut off from their unit for nine days.

12

2 Uniform, Combat Dress and Battle Equipment

Uniform

Although widely reported in the press of Western European countries, stories of German parachutists disguised as civilians operating in the Low Countries in 1940 were untrue; and rumours of German troops wearing British uniforms in Crete were equally lacking in substance. Dummy parachutists, *Fallschirmpuppen*, effectively tried out in air-landing exercises at Luneburg in July 1939, were, however, dropped in Belgium in 1940 in order to mislead the defence into believing that parachutists were being employed in greater numbers than they actually were.

In the Ardennes in winter 1944 combat teams of specially trained English-speaking saboteurs, under the leadership of SS leader, Otto Skorzeny, operated with the SS Panzer divisions; but only some of them were dressed in Allied uniforms. Battle reports at the time persistently confused the SS sabotage mission with the airborne support operation under the command of *Oberst* von der Heydte, whose military objectives were quite different. The 'scratch' force of parachutists in that

Combat dress variants: above left, Norway 1940, early pattern plain olive green overall; centre, USSR 1941, winter camouflage smock and trousers; right, Germany 1942, new overall with camouflage printed green and brown – note the knee protectors and front-lacing boots.

13

action wore standard combat dress but for many years the belief persisted that the operations were linked to the SS mission. The truth is that only by chance did *Oberst* von der Heydte learn of the Skorzeny operation. None of the SS men or their equipment were parachuted into action.

Much of the confusion over the rôle of parachutists in the early days in the West arose from the activities of a secret *Abwehr* unit that seized the Maas bridge at Gennep. The so-called 'tourists' from the Brandenburg Regiment were in fact dressed in civilian clothes. As 'tourists' they reconnoitred frontier defences in Belgium and Luxemburg. Their clandestine spying activities also extended into Holland and Northern France, where they contributed significantly to the state of alarm and war hysteria that gripped the West in 1940. .

The combat dress worn in action by parachute troops was quite different from that of any of the services of the Wehrmacht. The parachute rifleman's formal uniform as a member of the Luftwaffe was the ordinary air force uniform with yellow georgette patches and the name of the regiment was embroidered on the cuff, but this uniform was never worn in action.

Cuff titles in light green were authorised for Parachute Regiment 1 (FJR 1) in August 1939 and later for FJR 2 and were worn by all members of these units on the lower right sleeve. Other personnel of 7th Air Division, including the school at Stendal, wore the dark green Parachute Division cuff title. This was embroidered in aluminium wire thread for officers and in similarly coloured ordinary thread for other ranks.

After the fall of Crete Hitler authorised the award of a special 'Kreta' cuff title to all ranks taking part in Operation 'Mercury', including the flying and naval units that served the parachutists during the period 19th-27th May 1941. The title was embroidered in golden yellow thread on a white ground between two palm emblems, with a narrow border of the same colour above and below the title. Holders of this award, who also received documentary confirmation in the form of a certificate signed by General Student, wore the title above the left cuff of the tunic or greatcoat.

Combat Dress

1. Trousers like ski trousers, long, loose and grey in colour, with button pockets on the sides of the thighs.

2. Helmet round in shape, thickly padded with rubber, narrow brimmed, distinctive fork-shaped chin and neck straps and practically no neck shield. The Luftwaffe flying eagle insignia blazoned on the left side. In action the helmet was commonly worn with a plain or camouflage patterned cloth cover and frequently also with a self-coloured cross band for insertion of camouflage.

1

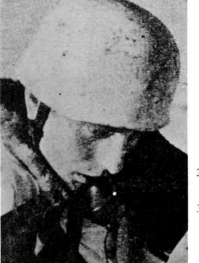

2

1. Combat dress and uniform detail, Norway 1940: standard pattern Luftwaffe service uniform. Note the collar patches denoting rank (yellow), map case, distinctive rimless helmet with forked chin strap and, on the background figure, the Fallschirmjäger bandolier.
2. USSR 1941, standard pattern helmet painted white.
3. France 1944, standard pattern helmet worn with cotton twill cover incorporating a band for inserting camouflage. Late pattern overall.
4. France 1944, standard Fallschirmjäger helmet worn without cover. Note the chin strap detail and Luftwaffe eagle printed on left side.

3   4

Normandy 1944, Hauptmann, right, in late pattern overall conversing with an orderly. Note the zippered pockets, camouflage helmet covers, map cases and, on the background figure, an army issue camouflage patterned poncho.

Germany 1939, Feldwebel in standard issue plain gabardine overall. Note the zippered thigh and chest pockets, leather holster for pistol 08 (Luger) and standard pattern helmet with forked chin strap.

3. A weatherproof gabardine overall, loose fitting and fastened with a zip fastener at the front. Worn over the uniform and webbing equipment for the jump, after dispensing with the parachute harness on landing the overall was taken off and put on again under the webbing equipment. Originally plain olive green, later (1940), issued with a camouflage pattern, the overall was cut short at the knees. Long sleeves buttoned at the wrist. The overall was provided with two capacious thigh pockets and two extra pockets on the chest.

1.

2.

3.

4.
Uniform detail 1939.
Left, practice in
boarding a JU 52.
Note the special
gauntlets, side-lacing
boots (pre-Crete) and
the static line gripped
between the teeth.
On command 'make
ready' the 'D' ring at
the end of the line is
clipped to a cable
running inside the
length of the fuselage.
Detail 1 Gauntlets,
2 Knee bandage,
3 Rubber soled boots,
4 Front-lacing boots,
post-Crete.

4. Boots, side lacing, of heavy leather and with thick rubber soles. Trousers tucked into the boots. After Crete boots were made front lacing.

5. Long gauntlet gloves of padded leather, rubber knee protectors. Linen bandages were worn to protect the ankles on landing.

17

Italy 1944, Below, Fallschirmjäger in tropical cotton drill shirt interrogating an Italian army sergeant. A standard pattern twelve compartment bandolier is slung around the neck. The rifle is the 98K, 7.92 calibre.

Italy 1943, right, Fallschirmjäger from the Demonstration Battalion pose for a group photograph after the successful freeing of Mussolini. Note the eight compartment bandolier for the FG 42, worn by the centre man. His companion, right, carries a grenade bag slung around the neck. The rifle is fitted with a grenade discharger cup. Compare the late uniform detail and equipment in this photograph with the detail in an earlier group photograph on page 20.

6. Bandoliers. A special twelve compartment bandolier carrying 120 rounds of standard 7.92 mm. rifle ammunition was issued to other ranks. Worn around the neck, the bandolier was secured by ties to the belt. For the FG 42, issued later in the war, the bandolier consisted of eight compartments only.

Badges and Identification: A special identity card was carried in the air force tunic pocket and an identity disc was worn around the neck. Pay books were handed in at the home station and not carried on operations.

Badges of rank, large size bars and wings on a yellow background, were worn on both sleeves of the overall; on the right breast was the Luftwaffe eagle (*Hoheitszeichen*). The parachutist badge, a diving golden coloured eagle in a wreath of silver oxidised oak and bay, was only worn on the formal Luftwaffe uniform. Every precaution was taken to conceal the movement and identity of parachute and glider-borne troops before an operation. Security measures even included banning the singing of paratrooper songs; and special equipment was concealed to best advantage and consigned separately from actual troop movements to airfields.

GERMAN AIR FORCE: INSIGNIA OF RANK *(Collar patch, shoulder strap, and coverall insignia)*
GENERAL OFFICERS *(Generale)*

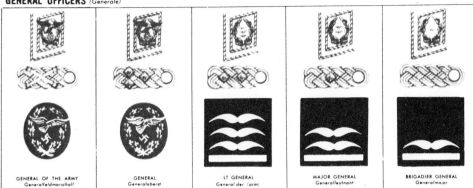

| GENERAL OF THE ARMY *Generalfeldmarschall* | GENERAL *Generaloberst* | LT GENERAL *General der (arm)* | MAJOR GENERAL *Generalleutnant* | BRIGADIER GENERAL *Generalmajor* |

FIELD OFFICERS *(Stabsoffiziere)*   COMPANY OFFICERS

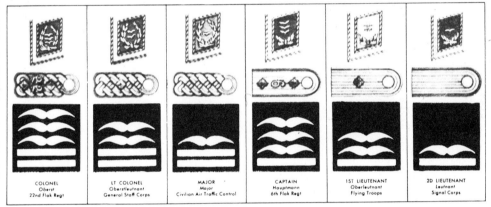

| COLONEL *Oberst* 22nd Flak Regt | LT COLONEL *Oberstleutnant* General Staff Corps | MAJOR *Major* Civilian Air Traffic Control | CAPTAIN *Hauptmann* 6th Flak Regt | 1ST LIEUTENANT *Oberleutnant* Flying Troops | 2D LIEUTENANT *Leutnant* Signal Corps |

NONCOMMISSIONED OFFICERS—TITLES:
Antiaircraft: Hauptwachtmeister, Oberwachtmeister, Wachtmeister, Unterwachtmeister
Other Units: Hauptfeldwebel, Oberfeldwebel, Feldwebel, Unterfeldwebel

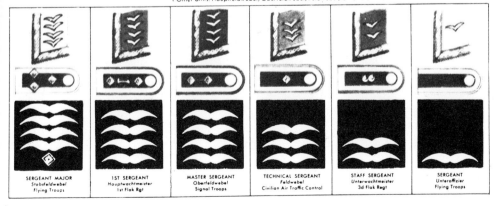

| SERGEANT MAJOR *Stabsfeldwebel* Flying Troops | 1ST SERGEANT *Hauptwachtmeister* 1st Flak Rgt | MASTER SERGEANT *Oberfeldwebel* Signal Troops | TECHNICAL SERGEANT *Feldwebel* Civilian Air Traffic Control | STAFF SERGEANT *Unterwachtmeister* 3d Flak Regt | SERGEANT *Unteroffizier* Flying Troops |

PLATE XI

A page from a US War Department manual illustrating German Air Force insignia of rank March 1945. Collar patches and shoulder straps varied in colour according to the arm of the service. Eg. Flak personnel pink, Signallers brown, Fallschirmjäger yellow.

Belgium 1940, a Fallschirmjäger group photograph snapped after the successful attempt to capture the fortress of Eban-Emael. All are wearing standard pattern plain overalls, side-lacing boots and helmets without covers. The left hand man carries a MP 38 machine-pistol and a grenade bag; another member of the group, fourth along the line, carries a 98K rifle.

Battle Equipment

Equipment carried into action in Holland and Crete included the following:

On the person: pistol O8, with two full magazines, two machine-carbine ammunition pouches, jack-knife, large field dressing, handkerchief, full water bottle, matches, safety pins, message pad with celluloid cover (for NCO's), marching compass, field dressings, string, fine wire and nails, respirator, anti-gas case, binoculars and pocket torch, woollen gloves.

Haversacks were issued to all ranks, also a carrying frame-type rucksack, ground sheet, and a special parachutist ration. The ground sheet was strapped to the haversack, which contained the parachutist's cleaning, washing and shaving kit, knife, fork, spoon, oil can and other personal articles. The haversacks were dropped in the arms-containers, but the rucksacks followed with spare clothing later in the company baggage.

20

Rations sufficient for two days included preserved bread, assorted tinned foods, chocolate, rusks, sweet biscuits, thirst quenchers and cigarettes. Energen or Dextro-Energen tablets, a glucose preparation to produce energy and a Benzedrine-type drug to produce alertness were also issued if considered necessary.

Ammunition carried on the man included four packets of pistol ammunition, ten rounds of ordinary pointed ball ammunition and ten rounds of armour-piercing bullets with tungsten carbide core for use with the MG 34. Hand grenades were carried usually on the belt. Smoke grenades, anti-tank rifle magazines, Bangalore torpedoes, demolition charges and reserve ammunition for all arms were packed in the arms-containers. The arms-containers were dropped from the bomb racks of the Ju 52 simultaneously with each stick (section) of parachutists.

21

Parachutes: The RZ1, *Rückenpackung Zwangauslösung 1*, parachute model 1, and later versions, RZ16, RZ 20 and RZ 36, according to many of those who used them in the early days, caused excessive oscillation in gusty weather, were difficult to manage and required too much time for quick release on landing.

The RZ1, a half globe parachute of twenty-eight panels, was developed for the paratroopers by the Luftwaffe's experimental station at Rechlin. This early model remained in service until spring 1940. The new RZ16 was introduced with improved static line packing. With the RZ1 the static line had sometimes impeded the release of the parachute and the full development of the canopy. Results were usually fatal.

Improvements to the central release catch were incorporated into the RZ20. Employed operationally for the first time in Crete, this model served until mid-1943. The later version, RZ36, was based at first on the Russian square-shaped parachute, but later assumed a triangular shape. This parachute caused considerably less oscillation and was easier to manage. The RZ36 became operational in October 1943. Few opportunities subsequently arose for this parachute to be used in action.

Parachutes were originally white in colour but operational experience in Holland revealed that white canopies were too conspicuous when lying collapsed on the ground. A camouflage pattern model was introduced, but officers continued to use white canopied parachutes so that they could be used as markers. 'Eye-witness' reports from the Battle of Crete speak of violet, red and other coloured parachutes being used but these reports are without foundation. Confusion may have arisen from the use of coloured smoke canisters attached to arms-containers for rapid identification of unit equipment.

Regimental commanders attached great importance to the rigging of parachutes – every man had to rig his own – resulting in valuable time being lost both in training and prior to an operation.

Pre-1940 training (opposite page). The early parachute was very conspicuous by its white canopy. The Wehrmacht decal is printed on the right side of the helmet.

Crete 1941: a new and less conspicuous camouflaged canopy hanging shroudlike above a dead Fallschirmjäger. Note the distinctive herringbone pattern of the rubber-soled boots.

23

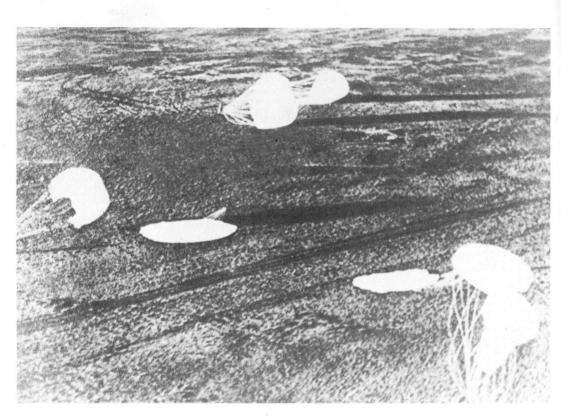

Inviting retribution.
White canopies signal
the presence of
airborne troops.
Without command of
the air this detachment
would suffer instant
retaliatory action
from enemy air forces.

In general German parachutists did not jump in training or on operations if the surface wind exceeded 14 mph. Operations attempted into a wind of greater velocity resulted in severe injuries and delayed the assembly of landed troops for hours. In order to minimize the time spent by the parachutist in descent, the jumping altitude was usually only 300-400 feet. (Higher jumping altitudes resulted in greater dispersion on the ground.) This was about as low as the Luftwaffe dare drop the parachutists; but lower altitudes were attempted in exceptional circumstances. In a well-trained unit using the transport (Ju 52) flying at 100-120 mph on the 'run-in' to the dropping zone, the despatch of twelve men could be accomplished in seven seconds. This would mean a fairly compact grouping with a distance of about 20 yards between the men on the ground. Experimental jumps were made in bad weather and in fog and systematic training in night jumping after 1942 produced satisfactory results, although only one night operation was actually carried out – in the Ardennes in late 1944.

Arms-Containers: *(Waffenbehälter)* were painted in various bright colours with rings and other unit markings and carried inside the Ju 52 transport plane. They were long canisters and were dropped from specially adapted racks in the bomb bay. The containers were packed according to the nature of their contents; but when guns were carried a specially fitted protective inner container was used.

Two or three different types were employed in Crete. A parachute

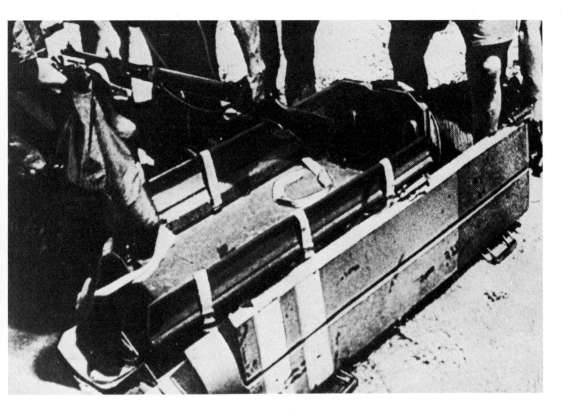

was attached at one end of the container which was released in the usual way by static line. To take the shock on falling on to hard ground the containers were provided with corrugated metal shock absorbers screwed to the bottom of the container. The shock absorbers were replaced if and when the containers were dropped a second time. Carrying handles were provided two on each side and a pair of bogie wheels, carried in the container itself, aided mobility on the ground. After landing two or even three containers were frequently dragged or towed one behind the other to an assembly area.

A section of twelve parachutists required four standard arms-containers when carried in a Ju 52. They were released at the same time as the men. Each weighed 50 lb. – 60 lb. empty or up to 260 lb. when loaded. Length: 5 feet. Diameter: 16 ins (approximately).

A single platoon of forty – fifty parachutists required fourteen arms-containers to carry their weapons and equipment into action. The only weapon with which the men jumped into battle at the time of Crete was the pistol and two magazines. Only the commanders of the first platoons to land carried machine-pistols with them. Dangerous delays, often fatal for the parachutists, were experienced in recovering their containers on the dropping zone. Consequently experiments were made in carrying machine-carbines, mortars, machine-gun ammunition and other equipment attached to the men in flight; thus improving the ability of the platoon to move off quickly into action.

Crete 1941: a standard arms - container with internal lining to absorb the shock of falling on hard ground is packed with small arms. Note the white painted rings at the near end of the container. They denote the section to which the weapons belong. After assembly containers are loaded into specially adapted bomb bays of a Ju 52 3M and will be dropped simultaneously with the section.

Italy 1943: the
standard infantry
weapon, MG 34
air-cooled belt-feed
machine-gun, used
widely by all German
armed services.
A standard pattern
entrenching tool and
bayonet is suspended
from the equipment
belt.

Holland 1945: the
MG 42, with a higher
rate of fire than the
MG 34, was issued to
Fallschirmjäger
companies during
1943. On the parapet
is a Panzerfaust
rocket ready for
action in a hand-held
launcher. Egg-type
hand grenades are
also at the ready.

3 Weapons

With the exception of the weapons discussed later, those carried by German parachute troops did not differ essentially from those of the infantry. Some changes were nevertheless made to standard infantry weapons. For example, the barrel of the infantry 8.1 cm. mortar was reduced in length in order to produce a manageable support weapon. This weapon was known as the *Stümmelwerfer* and paratroop battalions each had mortar companies equipped with both the 8.1 cm. and 10.5 cm. mortars.

Crete emphasised the need for 'heavy' backing in the shape of armour and artillery, the latter requirement being partially met by the introduction of 'light' guns; but a tank that could be carried on airborne operations never materialized. Experiments begun in 1942 on a two-man tank to be lifted in a large troop-carrying glider were discontinued because the general armaments situation did not allow sufficient opportunity for experimental development work.

Italy 1943: the 8.1 cm. mortar proved invaluable when supporting attack or defence. Three high explosive or smoke bombs were carried in each box.

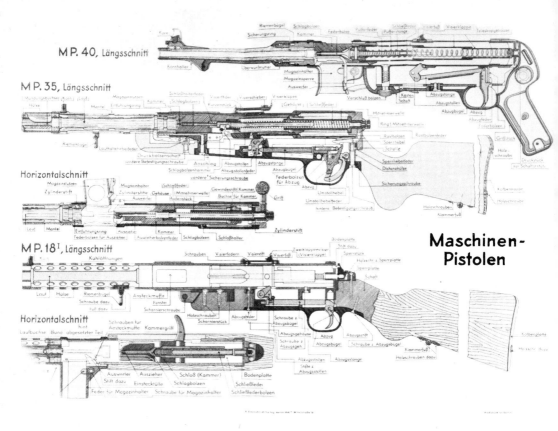

MP. 40, Längsschnitt

MP. 35, Längsschnitt

Horizontalschnitt

MP. 18¹, Längsschnitt

Horizontalschnitt

Maschinen-
Pistolen

MP 38 Machine-Carbine

A page from a
German weapon
training manual
illustrating the more
common machine-
pistols in police and
service use during
1943.

Until its replacement by a specially designed weapon the most famous 'symbol' of the parachute troops was the Erma MP 38 and its later variant, the MP 40. Both were of standard Wehrmacht issue. The MP 38 had been developed as a sub machine-gun for the army in the years between the First and Second World Wars. Full production was started in 1938 and continued until the end of 1942. The weapon and its later variant were each fed by a thirty-two round detachable box magazine using 9 mm. ammunition. The weight of the weapon was 9.5 lbs and barrel length 9.9 ins. The rate of automatic fire was 500 rounds per minute; no single shots were possible.

When jumping the weapon was either slung to the paratrooper's chest or broken up and stuffed in their overalls. The latter practice was inadvisable if the men were likely to face a hot reception on the dropping zone. In Crete some of the parachutists were obliged to open fire before hitting the ground. The weapon was alternatively dropped in the arms-container.

The lack of an adequate safety catch meant that the weapon was likely to go off when loaded and cause unnecessary accidents. Spare magazines were carried in distinctive, elongated leather or canvas pouches, usually worn on the equipment belt, three to each side. Each pouch carried two magazines.

28

Sicily 1943: ideal for street fighting, the MP 40. Stick grenades are carried in a satchel. Note the elongated pouches for the thirty-two round box magazine.

For the airborne troops the great disadvantage of this weapon was its non-standard use of 9 mm. ammunition. (The standard calibre was 7.92 mm.) This defect was not remedied until the introduction in 1944 of a specially designed weapon, the *Fallschirmjäger-Gewehr*, FG 42.

The special Fallschirm-Gewehr 42 with carrying sling, introduced into service with parachute companies during 1943. This model is fitted with a telescopic sight.

FG 42 Automatic Rifle

This was the only special type of small arms weapon expressly developed for use by parachute troops and used the standard infantry ammunition (7.92 mm.). The FG 42 entered service in 1943. The barrel length was 19.75 ins. A gas-operated weapon capable of automatic fire or single shots, the weapon when fired automatically equalled the rate of fire of the MG 42. The length of each burst was limited however to

Normandy 1944: in the close country around St Lô the fire power of parachute companies was greatly improved by the new short range weapon. This late production variant has a metal shoulder butt and wooden hand stock.

the extent of the twenty-round detachable box magazine. An extending bayonet was fitted for close quarter fighting and a telescope sight further enhanced the automatic rifle's usefulness. The weight was 9.93 lbs and bipod legs afforded stability when the weapon was used as a light machine-gun.

Germany 1940: a motor-cycle combination used in trials to tow the 3.7 cm. anti-tank gun into action.

PZ B.41 Anti-Tank Gun

As a special weapon for anti-tank fighting the paratroops in 1942 were given a tapered bore gun derived from the infantry version introduced into the army in 1941. The principal differences between the two versions were a lighter mounting, smaller balloon-type wheels and the elimination of the gun shield affording a saving in weight of some 200 lbs. More practical than the 3.7 cm. anti-tank gun, the new weapon unfortunately proved less successful than was anticipated against British heavy tanks, and after 1943 production was discontinued.

East Front 1941: the PzB41 with a forward company. This army model was later withdrawn and replaced by the 3.7 cm. anti-tank gun. Note the platform soles worn under the army issue boots.

Support Weapons

The need to deliver heavy support weapons and anti-tank guns into the hands of fighting airborne units; and once on the ground, the means of providing those units with ways of moving their guns into action, constantly occupied the attention of the air staff of 7th Air Division and later XI Air Corps.

The mountain gun (Gebirgskanon 36) of 7.5 cm. calibre was selected by 7th Air Division as a basic weapon for the artillery company and experimental use was made of Rottweiler dogs and Haflinger ponies to move the gun. The idea of using dogs was soon dropped. The ponies were expected to lie down in flight and remain cool under fire, but were generally difficult to manage. In action at Waalhaven airfield in Rotterdam, the animals broke loose and the ensuing chaos did not contribute to the efficient handling of the weapons.

31

Delivery was limited by the lifting capabilities of transport planes, particularly the Ju 52, whose limited internal load capacity greatly restricted the transport of heavy weapons. 10.5 cm. medium guns, 15 cm. howitzers and the horses necessary to haul them could not be delivered by parachute to the airborne troops. Even the 7.5 cm. mountain gun required several transport planes to land it in one piece.

The organisation and supervision necessary for the efficient packing and loading of heavy weapons and equipment at emplaning centres was provided in the shape of specially trained staff – *Verlastungskommandos.* Men, weapons and equipment were separated into 'loading units'; *Verladeeinheiten,* each unit being loaded on to one Ju 52.

During the attack on Holland, the number of loading units required for just part of an artillery regiment, and the problem of setting them down on the ground, so that loading units constituted a complete fighting unit may be gauged from the following extract from a secret report on the action of Air Transport Group 9, *KGrzbV 9,* formed especially for the purpose of transporting heavy weapons.

Action 3

The task was to land a troop of Artillery Regiment 22 on Field I with 6 aircraft under the command of Captain Blechschmidt.

According to the Division the Field was in German hands. This was not the case although an inverted swastika was laid out. On the contrary there was strong ground defence on the field and it was furthermore impossible to land because of the amount of rubble lying around. Therefore a landing by one aircraft on Field II (beach) was accomplished where our own troops just landed could already be seen. The other 5 aircraft did not land because of the difficulties of terrain. There were no losses.

One solution of the problem of the delivery of heavy weapons was the development of two-, three-, even five-fold parachute units for dropping a variety of weapons and equipment. In this way light recoilless 10.5 cm guns were dropped as a single unit, as was also the towing vehicle – a heavy motorcycle and sidecar. This latter vehicle was first packed in a metal frame, then suspended between the landing wheels of the transport and then dropped. But with the growing need to deal effectively with Allied armour, heavy weapons, such as the 75 mm. anti-tank gun demanded a 2-ton prime mover. Only the Me 323 Gigant powered glider produced in October 1942 was capable of transporting the gun and the glider was not operational until the latter part of the war.

Light Recoilless Artillery

The development of the *Leichtgeschütz* (light gun) used by German parachutists as a substitute for heavy weapons can be traced to the Krupp factory. Early experimental work lead in 1940 to the production of a 7.5 cm. model – LG 1. More efficient and heavier models employing the same recoilless principle of emitting part of the propellant gas to the rear were developed as the war progressed. As late

Italy 1943: 7.5 cm. anti-tank gun in firing position. The crew of four and their gun were transported from France in the giant Me 323 glider. A small towing vehicle was needed to move the gun into action.

France 1943: this photograph of a 10.5 cm. light recoilless gun and crew of three (they are, from left to right, loader, layer and commander respectively) was probably taken in France on a training exercise before the move from Istres to Italy.

France 1943: a second view of the 10.5 cm. light gun issued to parachute artillery companies.

as 1944, a 15 cm. model was planned as a substitute for the heavy infantry gun s. lG33.

Short barrels and light metal mountings gave the 'light' guns highly-prized mobility. This and their rapid rate of fire – respectively, eight and six rounds per minute – quickly endeared them to the paratroopers. In suitable terrain the 7.5 cm. gun could easily be hauled by two men; its range was 5,600 yards and that of the heavier 10.5 cm. gun was 8,600 yards. The latter model was introduced in 1943.

Both guns suffered the disadvantage of generating a large amount of smoke and fumes and the backflash was visible at night for a considerable distance. Attempts to use them as high-angle weapons (howitzers) were not satisfactory, but mountain troops and infantry to whom they were also issued found them highly effective against Yugoslavian partisans in the mountains of Serbia.

Other Weapons and Signal Equipment

A magnetic anti-tank hand grenade (*Panzerhaftladung*) was tried out as a special weapon for fighting tanks at close range only to be displaced by the universally adopted anti-tank grenade launcher (*Panzerfaust*). Some engineer units were equipped with the one-thrust flame thrower (*Einstossflammenwerfer*) developed for the SS, a more practical weapon than the cumbersome army flame thrower.

A signal pistol, also capable of firing smoke and anti-tank grenades, was introduced into service in 1942, but was soon withdrawn after proving highly dangerous to the careless user.

For their signals equipment the parachutists relied on the army's 'Dora' and 'Friedrich' radio sets. They proved very successful on airborne operations for voice communication on the ground, and contact by wireless telegraphy with rear echelons.

Parachute engineers
and signallers, like
their army counter-
parts, usually received
reliable equipment.
The examples
illustrated were issued
as standard equip-
ment to engineer and
signals companies.

above, Normandy,
1944: a field radio set
provides a link to
Bn HQ.

below, Holland,
1945: the flame-
thrower was often
useful as a defensive
weapon, especially
for clearing houses
during street fighting.

The mainstay of German transport operations, above, a
Ju 52 'workhorse' on a makeshift airfield in the Mediterranean
theatre. Below, a Go 242 twin-boom rear-loading glider,
introduced in 1942, photographed over the Rhone delta.

4 Air Transport

The Ju 52, affectionately known to the German paratroopers as 'Auntie Annie' or 'Judula', was a key factor in the development of German airborne forces and their early war-time operations. The German creation of an airborne corps was in fact built around the Ju 52: the standard three-engined Luftwaffe transport and supply plane employed on all fronts from 1939-1945; used also as the towing plane for the DFS 230 and Gotha 242.

Several thousand planes in the 3M production series were produced in five variants incorporating successive improvements such as additional armaments, automatic pilot and a more powerful radio. The plane seated a crew of three plus seventeen passengers or alternatively plus twelve parachutists and four containers in the bomb bay. The first military two-engined version of the Ju 52/3M flew in 1934 and was intended for use as a heavy bomber. This early version served by a crew of four, was armed with two 7.9 mm. machine-guns, one of which was

A DFS 230, the first German service glider, used at Eban-Emael and later in Crete, towed by a Ju 57B.

Heinkel III B's in towing formation, though rarely used in this capacity. Such powerful machines were unnecessary and could only infrequently be spared from bombing operations.

fitted in the now familiar dorsal position, the other being slung below the fuselage to provide protection for the belly and tail. 450 such machines entered service in the Luftwaffe, but little use was made of them. Developments in bombing techniques and the need for more sophisticated planes rendered them obsolete and by 1938 the Dornier Do 17E and Heinkel He 111B had replaced them.

Prior to the Second World War the Ju 52 enjoyed several thousand hours of civil flying in the service of Lufthansa and with many other of the world's airlines as well. As military planes, they saw service in the Condor Legion, a mixed force of bomber, fighter and reconnaissance planes sent by the Luftwaffe to support Franco in the Spanish Civil War. The rugged, tubular steel and corrugated aluminium skin construction of the Ju 52 proved of exceptional reliability. Three BMW radial engines rating 660 HP at sea level supplied the power. Speed reached 182 mph at 3,250 feet and the Ju 52 enjoyed a maximum range of 800 miles. When employed in transport and glider operations the ventral MG position was dispensed with and the undercarriage strengthened. Production continued until 1944, reaching its peak in 1942 with 887 machines. Approximately 3,000 planes were produced during the period 1939-1945, but by the end of that time only 150 remained in service.

The first air transport unit to collaborate with parachutists and to experiment with them in techniques of loading, navigation practice, jumping and general organisation was IV Group of *Kampfgeschwader* (bomber group) 'Hindenburg'.

This unit alone of those equipped with Ju 52's in 1936 was intentionally spared the need to re-equip with planes more suitable for the bombing rôle. In the year that Göring ordered the formation of the first German parachute battalion IV Group was earmarked for special assignment to the Air Commander Berlin, Luftwaffe *Generalmajor* Ulrich Grauert.

The intention of the air staff was to use this unit as a basis for future expansion of air transport units required for airborne operations. In October 1937 the unit was re-named *Kampfgruppe zbV1* – battle group for 'special purposes 1'. The use of the word 'special' was intended to stimulate the morale of the personnel of a unit ostensibly lacking in the traditional reputation associated with bomber and fighter groups.

Shortly thereafter responsibility for the group was shifted to 7th Air Division under *Generalmajor* Student, who was responsible for the development and co-ordination of airborne operations. The air transport group was placed directly under the command of the operations section of the divisional staff. At the same time a second air transport

Ju 52B on the East Front. A fatigue party helps to clear the machine for take-off. Many isolated units owed their survival to the resupply and air-dropping operations of the transport Geschwader.

Winter camouflage protects a 'Judula' at Schaikowka. Embattled units of the Assault Regiment defended the airfield against repeated Russian attacks throughout the winter of 1941-42.

group – Kampfgruppe zbV2 – was formed at Brandenburg-Briescht by transferring a cadre of personnel from *KGrzbV1*, the original air transport unit stationed at Fürstenwalde.

Organisation and equipment of both battle groups were expanded to match the growth in the establishment of the parachute units of 7th Air Division. Each transport group comprised four *Staffeln* (squadrons), each with twelve Ju 52's plus a staff-flight with five further planes, making a total of fifty-three planes in each group. A single group was thereby able to lift one parachute battalion of approximately 600 men.

Further growth of the parachute units to regimental strength *(Fallschirmjäger-Regiment 1)* created a need for two further transport groups. Soon a wing *(Kampfgeschwader)* with headquarters staff was brought into existence in order to maintain effective control of these groups. The new wing was established with a combined strength of four groups, a total of 220 planes and was designated *Kampfgeschwader zbV1*.

At the start of the Polish campaign in autumn 1939 this lone wing was joined by a second wing; equipped with Ju 52's drawn from the flying schools and swiftly made ready to transport the newly formed FJR 2. Simultaneously a special group *(KGrzbV9)* was created for the transport of heavy weapons.

40

The air transport groups employed by *KGzbVI* and *2* committed in the occupation of Denmark and Norway under command of Air Transport Chief, *Oberst* von Gablenz, totalled roughly 500 planes. During these first war-time missions, few losses were sustained; but in Holland the losses incurred were so great that some units losing as much as 90 per cent: of their operational strength were subsequently disbanded. Altogether, 186 transports were lost from a total of 430 actually employed in the operation.

The Dutch airfields, particularly in The Hague area, were littered with burnt-out and shattered transports: many of them drawn from the flying training schools together with their flying instructors; of whom a high percentage were peace-time volunteers, whose experience was impossible to replace at that time. Commander of *KGzbVI* was *Oberst* Morzik and that of *KGzbV 2 Oberst* Conrad, later appointed *Fliegerführer* of XI Air Corps. Morzik later succeeded von Gablenz as Chief of Air Transport Operations. Both groups had earlier trained and cooperated with 7th Air Division and 22nd (Air-Landing) Division. The vital ground organisation and techniques of loading and transporting a mixed airborne force of parachutists and air-landing troops, as well as the systematic co-ordination of flight procedures had gradually been perfected in many practice exercises.

For the invasion of Britain (Operation 'Sealion') the transport groups, some equipped with a specially developed giant glider Me 321, were built up to their former strength again and concentrated on airfields near Lyon, Lille and Arras. As events turned out they were not required, but Operation 'Mercury' took them southwards to the Greek airfields and planes also flew daily transport sorties in support of Twelfth Army in the Balkans campaign.

For the attack on Crete ten battle groups of *KGzbV 1* (*Oberstleutnant* Wilke), *KGzbV2* (*Oberst* von Heyking) and *KGzbV 3* (*Oberst* Buchholz), with roughly 500 transports, together with three special glider-towing groups of *LLG 1* – *Luftlandegeschwader 1* – for use by the Assault Regiment, were assembled in the neighbourhood of Athens under the command of XI Air Corps. Overall command of the operation was the responsibility of 4th Air Fleet under General Löhr.

Many of the departure airfields earmarked for the 'Mercury' transport groups lacked metal runways and were virtually cut-off from nearby Athens. The airfields at Elevsis, Tanágra, Dadion, Topolis, Mégara, Phaleron and Corinth, in the words of *Oberst* Heyking, commander of *KGzbV 2* were 'nothing but deserts'. During the Cretan operation heavily laden planes sank up to their axles in soft sand, sending clouds of dust skywards to a height of 3,000 feet. In these chaotic conditions vain attempts were made to lay the dust with water sprayed from carts. The transports were regrouped at opposite ends of the airfields; but the dust clouds shrouding take-off operations prevented the overhead assembly of the first transports by one hour for the 200-mile journey to Crete, and the turn-round for the second and third lifts were greatly hindered.

The petrol required to fill the tanks of the transport planes for Operation 'Mercury', some 650,000 gallons, was brought by tanker to isolated Piraeus through the Corinth Canal, now cleared of the remains of the former bridge by divers flown in from Germany; then transported in 45-gallon drums by truck to the airfields along the coast, where they finally arrived on 17th May, three days before the airborne assault was scheduled to begin.

After dropping parachutists in two waves on 20th May 1941 and transporting units of the mountain division on the following day, 200-250 supply missions were flown to the Mediterranean island; but after 30th May seaborne tenders took over the task of supplying the ground forces. On return flights from Crete after the capture of Máleme, empty planes were filled with casualties and flown back to Athens.

At one stage at Máleme airfield, as earlier at The Hague, wrecked planes were piled up on the runway and scattered throughout surrounding areas. Eighty broken and shattered machines obstructed the airfield. A captured British tank used as a bulldozer cleared them from the path of incoming flights. 271 transports were lost from the force of roughly 500 planes committed in the Battle of Crete.

After Crete, air transport operations in support of XI Air Corps were limited mainly to the ferrying of units into Tunisia in 1943, and later the lifting of 1st and 2nd Parachute Divisions into Sicily and the Rome area in 1943. No battle actions on the scale of Operation 'Mercury' were undertaken ever again; but plans were prepared for projected invasions of Malta and Gibraltar.

The air transport groups reverted to urgent 'airbridge' supply and reinforcement operations in Russia and with other newly-raised transport units later assisted in the evacuation of the Kuban in South Russia. Denied the opportunity of practising with the airborne corps, the transport groups gradually lost their special skills in battle formation flying and dropping parachute troops.

The glider towing unit 1/LLG1, established in 1939 with He 45, He 46 and later HS 126's, used in Crete for towing the DFS 230, was also withdrawn from the command of XI Air Corps and employed on the Eastern front to land supplies and equipment to encircled German units at Cholm, Welikiji, Luki and Tarnopol.

The Me 321 Gigant gliders developed for Operation 'Sealion' were formed into four squadrons in June 1940; and these gliders, too, were later employed on the Eastern front on supply and reinforcement missions. At the end of 1941 a new freight glider, Gotha 242, entered squadron service and proved invaluable for air transport operations in the years that remained of the war.

In October 1942 appeared the Me 323 Gigant six-engined powered glider, entering service with two transport groups –*I and II Gr/KG323zb V* – performing notable service for the airborne troops by transporting 1st and 2nd Parachute Divisions and their equipment from the South of France to Italy during July 1943.

Supply operations in North Africa, the Mediterranean and Eastern theatres of war took tremendous toll of the slow-moving Junkers and equally slow Me 323's. Losses in ground staff and equipment, too, were heavy, continually reducing the viability of the transport groups until in

Me 323, a cavernous six-engined transport developed from the Me 321. An 88 mm. gun and its prime mover are loaded experimentally at an airfield in southern Germany. Many of these slow moving transports fell to Allied fighters during the air-bridge operations between Sicily and Tunisia in 1942.

Rear-loading Go 242 on the airfield at Istres, the focal point for the German airborne troops deployed as strategic reserve in the Rhône delta. Both Fallschirmjäger divisions were transported from this airfield to Sicily and Rome in July or September 1943.

winter 1944 it was barely possible to scrape together the transports and trained pilots needed for the Ardennes operation. The resulting fiasco, a tragic parody of their earlier successes, marked the end of air transport operations in the service of the *Fallschirmjäger*.

In addition to the Ju 52 transport discussed earlier, other types of planes already mentioned in the text were occasionally used as transports and towing machines. These planes and the principal glider types employed in German airborne operations are now discussed in detail in the remaining part of this section.

France 1944: a late
variant of the DFS
230. The dorsal
machine-gun position
was intended for
defence in flight and
to keep down enemy
heads on the landing
zone. Note the
tubular steel
construction.

DFS 230: Developed prior to 1939 the DFS 230 entered military service in 1940 as the standard air force freight and air-trooping glider. Seating was provided for ten fully equipped troops including a pilot who was also expected to fight on landing.

Later variants (A and B production series) incorporated anchor-type braking systems. A special version (C) equipped with rocket brakes was employed in the successful action to free Mussolini from the Gran Sasso Plateau (1943). The glider was frequently employed in operations to carry supplies to beleaguered troops, (for example, Budapest in 1944).

The DFS 230 was later developed as a diving freight glider with a braking parachute fixed to the stern. This enabled the machine to approach and land at a very steep angle. The towing line was originally of 5 mm. thick steel ply construction with a length of 40 metres; but this was superseded by a 4-metre long rigid tubular section towing link. This made a calmer flight possible.

Initially, development was the responsibility of the German Institute for Gliding Research (DFS), which at the instigation of Ernst Udet in 1933 received a contract to build a military version of its experimental meteorological observation machine, a wide wing span glider designed for high altitude flight. A prototype 230 duly appeared and by 1937 confidence in the design resulted in the first production series at the Gothaer vehicle factory.

44

Construction of the box-shaped fuselage was of tubular steel with canvas cover. The wings, entirely wood, were high set and braced. Flaps were fitted on the upper surface of the wings and opened upwards to steepen the angle of glide. Wheels were detachable and jettisoned on operational flights. Accommodation was rather cramped, seats being arranged in a single line, six facing forwards and four backwards. Instruments were limited to air speed indicator, rate of climb, turn and bank indicators and compass. Navigation and landing lights were operated from an accumulator fitted in the nose. Operational employment in Crete revealed the vulnerability of the DFS 230 to accurate ground fire.

Many machines suffered hits in the forward fuselage killing pilots and exploding reserve ammunition. Slow flight made the glider an easy target and many crews were killed in flight. Gliders broke up on landing on rocky terrain; but the great advantage of the DFS 230 was its almost noiseless approach to the battle zone; and its small measure of success was due largely to this factor.

USSR 1941: forerunner of the six-engined Gigant, this powerless model introduced for Operation Sealion is pictured at Orscha. The airfield there became an important centre for air transport operations on the central sector of the East front.

Me 321 – Gigant: This transport was introduced in 1941 for the projected invasion of Britain, Operation 'Sealion'.

Capable of lifting a small tank or 7.5 cm. anti-tank gun – or 200 men. Front door loading.

165 machines were built and held in readiness for Operation 'Sealion'; but they were subsequently transferred to the Eastern front and proved useful on supply and transport operations, particularly in the Riga-Orscha area. Three Me 110's were used in the so-called *Troikaschlepp*, but this hazardous three-point towing operation resulted in the death of many pilots.

Two views of the Me
323 Gigant; in flight
during trials in
Germany and later
unloading operations
at an unidentified
airfield, probably on
the East front (IWM).

Me 323 – Gigant: A supertransport developed from the 321 glider and introduced in 1942.
Crew of five. Powered by six Gnôme Rhône radial engines. Wing span 181 ft. Length 92 ft. 3 ins.

Early models provided with eight wheels, later increased to ten. Capable of lifting 130 troops or sixty wounded or 21,500 lbs of freight (three times capacity of the Ju 52).

Highly vulnerable due to low speed. Fourteen 323's fell prey to Allied fighters in a single action during the Tunisian supply operation in 1943. Several versions entered service in two production series (D and E). In 1943 the development of 323 was transferred to the Zeppelin Co., where a more powerful series (F) was projected but none became operational. The freight capacity covered one complete 8.8 cm. anti-aircraft/anti-tank gun.

He 111Z introduced in 1942 as a special towing machine for the Me 321 Gigant. Constructed from two standard He 111's, the machine was joined by a centre wing section in which three motors were installed. Two additional motors were provided on the port and starboard wings. This five-engined hybrid was produced only in small numbers and needed a crew of seven. Later variants in the Z series included bomber (4 x 1800 kg.) and radio reconnaissance versions.

Another view of the Go 242 taken by a colleague of the pilot on the East front, spring 1942.

Gotha 242 was introduced in 1942 as a freight glider and partly as a replacement for the smaller DFS 230.
Span: 72 ft. Length: 52 ft. Crew of two.

Capable of lifting twenty-one fully-equipped troops or equivalent freight.
Weight empty: 7,040 lbs. Weight loaded: 15,620 lbs. Rear loading ramp.

Improvements were introduced in several variants (A and B production series) and a special version was projected for use against the British fleet at Scapa Flow. A major development (Gotha 244) was brought about by equipping the 242 with two radial engines but this did not prove particularly successful and few entered service.

Gotha 345, introduced in 1944 as a freight glider, was subsequently projected for use as a ten-seat battle-glider equipped with two pulse modulated engines suspended from the wings. A braking rocket was fitted under the centre fuselage. The machine required a two-man crew. Later from the same Gotha works came the Gotha ka 430, a development of the 242 but only a handful of these machines were produced before the military situation brought production to a standstill. Other Gotha and DFS projects involved co-operation in the planning of a strategic glider (DFS 331) and a transport plane to incorporate easier loading and access facilities and greater capacity (Gotha P50) but none entered service.

Go 242 photographed
in North Africa,
probably late 1942.
Many German
service airfields were
overrun by British
and American troops
in their drive against
Panzer Army Africa.
Gliders such as this
were often captured
intact. (IWM)

Crete; British Army Intelligence gathered first hand information on German airborne operations and capabilities. This page from an Intelligence report on Operation Mercury illustrates the loading plan of a DFS 230 glider with three typical loads.

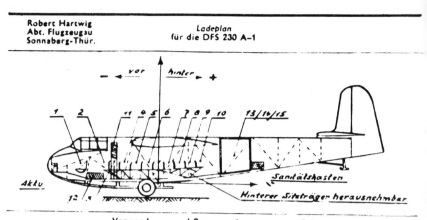

Robert Hartwig
Abt. Flugzeugbau
Sonneberg-Thür.

Ladeplan
für die DFS 230 A-1

vor   hinter

1   2   11 4 5 6   7 8 9 10   13/14/15

Akku

12

Sandsackkasten

Hinterer Sitzträger herausnehmbar

Verwendungs- und Beanspruchungsgruppe : P 3

Pos.	Benennung :	Verwendungszweck :		
		I Zugtrupp	II MG-Trupp	III Schützentrupp
	Leergewicht	780	780	780
	zus. Ausrüstung *)	32	32	32
	Rüstgewicht	812	812	812
	Zuladung :			
1.	Besatzung	70–100	70–100	70–100
2.	„	70–100	70–100	70–100
3.	„	70–100	70–100	70–100
4.	„	70–100	70–100	70–100
5.	„	70–100	70–100	70–100
6.	„	70–100	70–100	70–100
7.	„	70–100	70–100	70–100
8.	„	70–100	70–100	70–100
9.	„	70–100	70–100	70–100
10.	„	70–100	70–100	70–100
11.	6 Gewehre	23	23	23
12.	6 Munitionskästen (voll)	—	50	50
13.	1 schweres MG	—	36	—
14.	1 leichtes MG	—	—	13
15.	2 Funkkästen	35	—	—
	Fluggewicht	1.870 kg	1.921 kg	1.898 kg

Maxim. Fluggew.—Schwerpunktsvorlage : — 174 mm vor Hauptspant — 27%. to
„   „   „   Rücklage : — 15 mm „   „   — 33%. to

anmerkung :
Höchstzul. Fluggewicht 2100 kg.   Bei Alleinflug sind 60 kg Ballast auf Sitz Nr. 2 mitzunehmen.
Schwere Insassen haben bei voller Besatzung die Sitze Nr. 2, 3, 4, 5 usw. zu belegen. to-Flügeltiefe
in Symmetrie-Ebene (2, 8 m).   Vord. Punkt von to liegt — 0, 94 m vor Hauptspant.
*) siehe Beladevorschrift.

Bearbeiter :	Geprüft :		

Loading plan of the D.F.S. 230 glider.   This shows the ten seats (1-10), rifle rack (11), boxes of ammunition (12), and position of L.M.G. or W T set (13, 14, 15).   The four rear seats can be removed.   There is a first-aid box in the rear of the fuselage.   The maximum useful load is given as 1,288 kg. (2,834 lb. or rather over 1¼ tons).   Specimen loadings are given for the H.Q. Sec. (six rifles and W/T transmitter and receiver), M.G. Sec. (L.M.G. on heavy mounting, six rifles, and six boxes of ammunition), and rifle sec. (L.M.G., six rifles, and six boxes of ammunition) : compare the loadings given in Chapter II, 5.

5 Training and Organisation

German airborne troops during the period 1936-45 fell into three categories:

1. Gliderborne troops of the Luftwaffe landed from the air in gliders, principally the DFS 230. Used in 1940 in company strength at the Albert Canal and at Fort Eban-Emael and later in battalion strength as part of *Sturm Regiment 1* in Crete.

2. Parachute troops of the Luftwaffe transported and dropped from the air by the Ju 52. The original airborne formation was a single Parachute Rifle Regiment, *Fallschirmjäger-Regiment 1* (FJR 1) formed in 1936. At the end of the war expansion had led to a total strength of ten parachute divisions.

3. Air-landing troops flown in by Ju 52's after the glider and parachute troops had secured a suitable airfield or landing strip. They were army troops intensively trained and equipped for transportation by air. First used in battalion strength in the occupation of the Sudetenland in 1938, full divisions were later committed in Holland, *22. Infanterie (Luftlande) Division*, and Crete, *5. Gebirgsjäger Division*.

Gliderborne troops: Glider pilots were members of the Luftwaffe, although some may earlier have served in the army. Most were men with previous experience of civilian flying in gliders and many had been members of the German Glider Flying Association; reported as having some 50,000 members as early as 1932. Gliding was then a popular sport in Germany, particularly in the Wasserkuppe mountains southeast of Fulda, and in *'Fliegerkorps'* training centres such as Rhön where pilots could take 'A' and 'B' tests on gliders. Gliding was encouraged by the *Reichswehr* and later by the Nazis as quasi-military training in defiance of the Treaty of Versailles until Germany openly rearmed in the mid-1930's. Schools were established at Rossiten in East Prussia, Dörnberg near Kassel and Syat in Westerland.

The glider pilot's badge, a soaring eagle on a wreath of oak leaves with swastika was either embroidered or made of 'German' silver. Training on the large gliders was initially undertaken in conditions of great secrecy in preparation for the attack on the fortress of Eban-Emael. The training was carried out in the glider unit itself, the first of which was formed at Hildesheim near Hanover in November 1939 under the command of *Hauptmann* Koch.

France 1943: loading
equipment aboard a
DFS 230.

An important feature of the training was the making of spot landings
– in the case of Eban-Emael, directly on to the roof of the fortress. Blind
flying too was taught at the glider training school later established not
far from Hildesheim at Braunschweig-Weggum, where the course lasted
for six weeks. In addition to his flying training the pilot, in command
during the operational flight, received standard infantry training as he
was expected to fight on landing.

The pilot's training was not always undertaken in close conjunction
with the troops he was to transport or with the towing plane. Gliderborne troops, trained as infantry shock troops, learned to debouch from
their gliders and move quickly into action; their great advantage being
their close grouping and virtually silent approach to the landing zone.
Some were given parachute training. After 1942 all airborne troops were
trained for commitment by either glider or parachute. Gliderborne
troops were lifted in sections of ten men.

One glider squadron of twelve gliders was able to transport a company of 120 men in an airborne operation such as 'Mercury'. The glider
companies, four of which were employed operationally at the time of
Crete, were embodied in one battalion of an assault regiment which, as
its name implies, was to be used as the spearhead of the airborne attack.
1st Assault Regiment led by *Generalmajor* Eugen Meindl in the

52

operation consisted principally of four battalions each of four assault companies with a total regimental battle strength of 2,000 all ranks and 220 pilots. Close support for the assault companies was provided by heavy mortars, machine-guns and anti-tank guns. In Crete after intensive preliminary bombing the gliderborne companies landed fifteen minutes ahead of the parachute companies.

Parachute troops: Training for volunteers was originally given at Stendal some sixty miles west of Berlin; where in 1936 the newly formed *Fallschirmjäger-Regiment* (Parachute Rifle Regiment) had its headquarters. The first parachute training school was closed in December 1940 and transferred a little distance to the north to Wittstock and then westwards on the North West German plain to Braunschweig. The Braunschweig school too was later closed and new schools at Dreux near Paris and at Salzwedel on the present East German Border were opened in 1942. Later another school was opened at Kraljevo in Serbia.

After completing three months initial training in the handling of infantry weapons, entrants into the parachute training schools practised close combat techniques and handled enemy weapons and equipment. The sixteen-day parachute training course that followed included

France 1943: a Fallschirmjäger section boarding a Ju 52 for a training flight. The jump master (centre) is checking the position of the parachute. Each man takes the line between his teeth as he climbs into the aircraft, see next page.

Parachute packing was an individual responsibility practised frequently on a special table such as this one at Stendal in 1939.

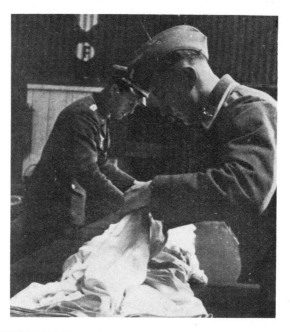

Stendal; a training officer using a megaphone corrects the landing posture of recruits at the parachute school.

lectures on parachute packing, aircraft drill, parachute flight control, rolling on the ground and 'throwing-off' the parachute harness. Instruction finally was given on movement inside the fuselage and on exits from a simulated Ju 52 trainer on the ground. Jumps were made in combat dress with full kit from a platform 3 metres high on to matting; practised for at least one hour a day. On the last six days of the course six training jumps were made from a Ju 52, including a company jump at 350 feet. Occasionally the Do 23 and Heinkel 111 were used on training flights.

Personal qualities demanded were toughness, physical fitness and mental alertness; preference was for specially aggressive volunteers whose training was primarily intended to bring out qualities of initiative and independence. All trainee parachutists were volunteers and officers, non-commissioned officers and men all went through the same form of training. They were encouraged to believe that they were superior soldiers. Two out of three failed the basic training course; but men seldom refused to jump once they finally reached the jumping training.

On approaching the dropping zone, the *Absetzer* (despatcher), usually a non-commissioned jumping instructor, on a signal from the pilot, alerted the men with the command 'make ready' and then sounded a klaxon as a warning for the men to prepare for action. The spring hook of their parachute pull-out cord or static line was clipped on to a steel cable running the length of the plane immediately below the roof; the alerted parachutists then shuffled swiftly towards the port door sliding back the hook along the cable. The stick was expected to make its exit in six or seven seconds. After the individual exit, when the man had fallen a short distance the static line jerked taught and broke open the parachute pack thus releasing the parachute canopy and rigging lines.

Unlike British paratroopers who dropped through a hole in the fuselage of various converted bombers and later in an upright position from the door of the Dakota, the *Fallschirmjäger* dived from the exit door with arms outstretched. Once the parachutist had fallen through the slip stream, and the parachute canopy was fully developed, a rapid assessment was made of the direction of descent. Unfortunately the means were not provided for controlling the parachute canopy in flight, but parachutists made an attempt to correct excessive rotation or pendulum movement by spread-eagling their limbs. Spread-eagling could be hazardous as it was essential for the feet and knees to be together on first contact with the ground. Simultaneously with hitting the ground the parachutist rolled over from the direction of approach to the ground. If a gust of wind filled up his canopy he was liable to be dragged some distance along the ground. If the parachutist experienced difficulty in extricating himself from his parachute harness, he cut himself loose with his jack-knife.

After six jumps the graduates received the parachutist's badge. Qualification for the badge after 1943 included at least one night jump. Organised in sections of twelve men, a parachute company's battle strength consisted of 144 officers and men. Three parachute rifle battalions each of three parachute rifle companies and a heavy company with mortars and machine-guns were organised into a parachute

Training at Stendal.
1. seconds after leaving aircraft the parachute canopy is released by a static line. This remains attached to the machine.
2. controlling the canopy on the ground is practised with the aid of an improvised wind machine.
3. waiting in flight for the command 'make ready' and then 'jump'.

France 1943: training of recruits at the parachute school at Stendal, later at Dreux, and elsewhere, was rigorous and thorough. Jumping and landing techniques were practised with the help of a mattress or hand-held trampoline. The Oberjäger, a Crete veteran, demonstrates the right way in which to adjust the parachute harness and the correct position for leaving the aircraft. The aperture is the same size as the doorway of a Ju 52. The artist's drawing is prewar, probably made in 1939 and published in an airforce magazine.

rifle regiment. Anti-tank and mountain guns were provided for the regiment in separate companies and allotted to companies or battle groups in accordance with their operational needs. The organisation of a parachute rifle regiment was similar to that of the ordinary infantry regiment. The great difference was the former's lack of heavy equipment.

The tactical method of employing parachute troops conceived by *Generaloberst* Student was his 'oil-spot' technique of dropping units in complete groups over a wide area and assembling them for action as rapidly as circumstances would permit. The basic operational unit of a parachute company could assemble in ideal conditions five-ten minutes after hitting the ground. Leaving their deflated parachutes behind, the men quickly collected their weapons from the containers dispersed on the dropping zone and organized themselves in groups in company rendezvous areas.

Before the drop intensive preliminary bombing and machine-gunning were directed against airfields, planes on the ground and AA gunsites by support wave squadrons of Stuka and fighter bombers. The 'run-in' was usually heralded by an intensification of these attacks and greatly increased low level machine-gun raids. Local enemy concentration areas and approach roads to the selected dropping zones were also methodically strafed. In Crete after one hour of incessant low level attacks the Ju 52 transports appeared and the first wave of gliders followed by parachutists then descended from the sky.

The first airborne troops to land laid out swastika flags as markers for successive waves of aircraft, and ground strip codes signalled messages to their support and resupply aircraft. (In Crete the defenders used captured strips to call for and receive a useful range of enemy equipment, including anti-tank guns, bicycles, stores and medical equipment.) Contact between units and the home base was established by wireless; and a well-organized, visual ground-air signal system enabled a specially trained observer with forward troops to communicate with spotter aircraft; thus achieving great accuracy in co-ordinating air strikes on enemy positions.

Air-landing troops: Infantry and mountain divisions of the Wehrmacht were earmarked for special training for transportation by air. They were to be committed once an aerodrome had been secured and the runway cleared to land. In practice only one such division, the 22nd (Air-Landing) Division, was ever fully trained and sent into action. A single regiment, IR 16, one of the three regiments belonging to this division, was used by the army in 1938 for a training exercise and as part of the 7th Air Division landed at Freudenthal during the occupation of the Sudentenland.

Prague airport was occupied by both army and Luftwaffe air-landing troops in March 1939. Oslo airport was similarly occupied just over a year later – over 3,000 troops landing within an hour. In 1940 22nd (Air-Landing) Division took part in the invasion of the Low Countries. But in Holland and later in Crete the Ju 52's were arriving whilst airfields were still under fire and only dust and smoke from exploding shells saved the air-landing troops from annihilation.

Men of the infantry and mountain divisions were organised in self-contained company groups; sixteen or even eighteen lightly equipped men being allocated to each plane. A light mountain gun (the Skoda 16) and six men required virtually three planes; one for the gun and its crew and two more for accessories with some room left for further personnel. When committed in Crete the mountain troops of 5th Mountain Division travelled with their equipment in sections of seven or eight men per Ju 52; whereas in Holland the personnel of 22nd Infantry Division had travelled with their equipment in sections of nine or ten men per plane. After Crete neither the 22nd nor any mountain divisions were ever used on airborne operations again.

Secret Report of Air Transport Group KGrzbV 9, on operations in Holland Operation 2

8 aircraft in two flights under the command of Captain Külbel and Captain Wildau had the task of setting down 8 loading units of the 14th Company of Infantry Regiment 65; about 70 men with 4 guns, without horses. It was forbidden to land on landing fields that were not unequivocally in our hands. Because Fields II and I and surroundings were under heavy fire the landing took place on Field IV Waalhaven. Shortly before the 4th aircraft of the 1st flight (9 + BH) was shot down and destroyed. The rest unloaded on the northeast side. The field was under artillery fire. In addition, English bombs with time fuses were exploding. As further bomb attacks were to be expected the return flight was not delayed. It passed without incident.

Start in Lippspringe 14.35 hours
Landing in Lippspringe between 18.30-18.45 hours

6 Military Operations — Early Days

The German attack on Crete on 20th May 1941 was to provide the most impressive demonstration of the German conduct of airborne operations in the Second World War.

In this operation the combined efforts of transport, fighter and Stuka groups, gliderborne and parachute troops of the Luftwaffe and air-landed army troops were committed with the support of seaborne landings in a bold plan to seize the island defences, manned by determined British, Dominion, Greek and Cretan soldiers and covered and protected by the Royal Navy.

Crete, although a triumph for German arms, nevertheless came within a hair's breadth of disaster. Demonstrating more convincingly than any of its limited precursors in Belgium and Holland that a large airborne contingent could successfully wage a new form of warfare, the Valkyrian descent on Crete followed the earlier triumph of German armoured troops in France. Although Russian parachutists had appeared on military manoeuvres since the early 1930's, prior to 1939 little or no thought had been given to the organisation of parachute forces by the British – or Americans, who were soon to join the war. In 1940 Winston Churchill ordered the raising of the first British paratroop formation; but it was not until Crete that Western military thinkers were jolted into considering the future rôle of airborne forces. Although Allied airborne operations too tasted triumph and disaster, their ideas were developed to such good effect that Allied paratroopers played an important part in the final eclipse of the Wehrmacht in North West Europe.

Men considered parachute descents from hot air balloons in the late eighteenth century, but the preamble to the story of the launching of the German sky battalions in 1940, should properly commence during the First World War. Artillery officers on both sides were much experienced in escaping by parachute when their captive kite balloons were destroyed by machine-gun or rifle fire. In the latter part of the war pilots made good use of the parachute when their planes were shot down in combat. Air forces landed or parachuted reconnaissance and sabotage agents behind both sides of the line. These operations from 1916 onwards were limited mainly to the use of one or more agents acting independently. One such instance in 1918 was the setting down by the Italians of four of their agents on a reconnaissance mission behind the Austrian lines.

Of greater significance on the Allied side was a plan by the American Colonel William 'Billy' Mitchell, later General Mitchell, to employ

2,000 planes in dropping a parachute division behind the Hindenburg Line and attack the city of Metz from the rear. Mitchell's plan was conceived in mid-1918 prior to the great autumn Victory offensive when the American Expeditionary Force in Lorraine was already committed to mounting operations in the general direction of Metz. Unknown to Mitchell and a junior officer – Lewis Brereton – the Metz Fortress had been stripped of its guns; but the means of achieving an airborne 'Cannae' in 1918 were non-existent. Colonel Mitchell's visionary plan, which failed to win support from General Pershing, the American commander-in-chief, was undoubtedly as advanced in concept as his daring ideas on the use of the aeroplane in the rôle of strategic air bombardment.

Undismayed, after the war General Mitchell pursued his interest in strategic air bombardment and airborne landing operations, and in magazine articles and a paper directed to the United States Air Staff in the early 1920's the General advanced his theories on vertical envelopment. His thesis was supported by a practical demonstration jump by six men making exits from a single plane on to Kelly's Field in Texas. These efforts were unhappily disregarded and the General was denied an opportunity of testing his ideas on a wider scale.

Elsewhere during the 1920's and early 1930's as military occasion arose in Europe or in the Middle East the armed forces of Italy, Britain and France experimented with transporting troops into action by air and during this period many useful advances were made in the development of parachutes and methods of air trooping.

The RAF introduced troop carrying planes into service in 1922, notably the Vickers Vernon, a descendant of the First World War Vickers Vimy bomber. In 1923 air-transported troops were lifted into action in Iraq in support of ground operations against dissident tribesmen. During the troubles of 1932 in the same area an infantry battalion was lifted by air from Egypt to reinforce the local garrison; a pioneering effort that regrettably failed to impress the senior echelons of the British military establishment.

No British parachute force in fact materialized until July 1940 when after noting in June the success of the German airborne assault on the Low Countries, Winston Churchill personally ordered the raising of a British parachute battalion. Accordingly the 11th Special Air Service Battalion (No 2 Commando) underwent parachute training under the Royal Air Force at Ringway near Manchester, thereby providing the nucleus of a British airborne force.

In the United States General Mitchell was still unable to win official support for his theories; and as a result of charges of incompetence levelled against his colleagues, Mitchell was court-martialled and obliged to resign from the army in 1926. Mitchell continued to advance his theories and warn against Japanese aggression: he died in 1936 but in 1942 was reinstated posthumously in the rank of major-general after his warnings and predictions had struck home. In 1941 a parachute group and school had been established at Fort Benning and serious experiments also started with gliders and air-landing techniques. At the beginning of the Second World War therefore neither Britain nor the

United States possessed viable airborne forces.

The Italian General Staff on the other hand welcomed new ideas and a collective drop by Italian parachutists was made near Milan in November 1927. Unlike the American hand-operated, rip-cord parachute already developed and used by Leslie L. Irvin in 1919 at Dayton, Ohio, the Italians were using a generally reliable parachute operated by a static line, also used by their pilots who hooked up before leaping from a doomed machine. Unfortunately General Guidoni, a leading Italian exponent of airborne operations, was killed a year later when his parachute failed to open. Experiments continued however and the Italians raised complete parachute battalions that were later expanded into the *Folgore* and *Nembo* divisions eventually earmarked in 1942 for the projected invasion of Malta. These first-class Italian divisions were destined never to take part in full scale airborne operations.

In France, where the mystique of *les paras* was to pervade the potentially powerful French army in the 1950's, two companies of *Infanterie de l'Air* were raised only to be disbanded before 1939. After the Second World War, France along with the USSR were pioneers in the development of the sport of free-fall parachuting on a tremendous scale.

Only in the USSR were firm foundations laid prior to 1939 for raising and employing airborne troops on a large scale. Parachutists took part in the Russian manoeuvres in 1930 and again during the following year in a small scale engagement against bandits in Central Asia. In 1935 and 1936 the Russians demonstrated on manoeuvres their technique of jumping *en masse* from four-engined transport aircraft, the first effective demonstration of the use of parachuting in a military rôle. Eye-witnesses and observers of newsreel film of the occasion in 1935 were intrigued to see the parachutists clambering on to platforms built on to the tail of the Ant-14 transport planes. After steadying themselves in an exposed and rather vulnerable position, the parachutists then hurtled into space reaching for the rip-cords of their manually operated parachutes.

Actually present at the 1935 demonstration was the future General Student, later the leading personality in creating the German airborne forces. Major-General, later Field-Marshal Earl Wavell also witnessed the demonstration by Russian parachute troops. Altogether 1,500 troops were successfully dropped with light arms and equipment. Unlike Student, Wavell left Russia with no appreciation of the true potential of airborne operations. Five years later he was British Commander-in-Chief Middle East with supreme responsibility for the defence of Crete.

That the Russians failed to exploit their early experiments in the 1930's was later to become only too evident with their lack of success with parachute formations during the Second World War. (Parachutists were however used successfully on a limited scale in conjunction with partisan forces.) Only in Germany did the airborne idea as developed before the war take root; thanks to the vision and dedication of a group of forward looking army and air force officers. The airborne armadas with which the Luftwaffe captured Crete in 1941 and with which Allied forces later spearheaded the Normandy invasion and the crossing of the Rhine owed a great deal to the pioneering endeavours of General Student and his colleagues.

A vital step in the implementation of German plans for the development of the airborne idea was the mass production of a reliable transport aircraft; the Junkers, Ju 52, introduced into airline service by Lufthansa in 1932 and already secretly intended for conversion to bombing and military transportation rôles. The merits of the Ju 52 and its place in the airborne concept have already been discussed; but mention must be made here of another rôle which this versatile plane was often called upon to perform.

The troop-carrying capacity of the Ju 52 was demonstrated early in the Spanish Civil War when a force of thirty of these planes assisted General Franco by lifting a total of 9,000 Moroccan troops and legionnaires, artillery, machine-guns and munitions across the Mediterranean from North Africa to Seville. The successful strategic redeployment of such a large force of men and materials altered the balance of power between opposing forces at a crucial stage of the battle then in progress.

The date generally regarded as the birthday of German airborne forces is 29th January 1936. On that day Hermann Göring, as Chief of Air Force and Air Transport Minister, issued orders for the raising of a parachute regiment (*Fallschirmjäger-Regiment 1*) with its first battalion, headquarters and training school situated at Stendal in North West Germany; volunteers were recruited from the Hermann Göring Regiment, formerly the Prussian state police. Commander of the regiment was *Oberst* Bruno Bräuer.

The army, too, was interested in exploring the potential of airborne operations and at Stendal also in the same year a parachute infantry company was formed and subsequently increased in size to a full battalion, *Fallschirm-Infanterie-Bataillon*. Commander of the army parachute battalion was *Major* Richard Heidrich.

As soon as the school at Stendal was set up in 1936, responsibility for the training and development of German airborne forces lay with *Major* F W Immans. In 1937 *Oberst* Bassenge was appointed to command the establishment. About this time technical development of the German parachute focussed upon the static line 'Salvator' type developed by the Italian air force. Experiments at Stendal had shown that manually operated parachutes were almost useless at altitudes of less than 600 feet. Training and operational requirements called for a dropping height of 300 feet; necessitating the rapid development of the parachute canopy, and for which purpose the automatic or static line method of opening the parachute was clearly the more suitable.

Bassenge, in furthering the ideas of the General Staff on the tactical employment of airborne troops, organised a demolition exercise in which fourteen squads were dropped by parachute to attack railway installations and communications in 'enemy' areas. Adolf Hitler and senior officers present at the demonstration were greatly impressed; but as yet no firm policy existed for the systematic organisation and employment of this new arm of the Wehrmacht.

The Colonel's demonstration carried out by teams drawn from the Hermann Göring Regiment confirmed the speed and effectiveness with which sabotage operations could be performed by parachutists. A platoon from the SS also underwent parachute training, the SS intention being to form a cadre for a future SS parachute formation.

In anticipation of the march into Czechoslovakia in 1938 Colonel Bassenge was instructed to alert his paratroopers and to include among them a contingent from the SA *Sturmabteilung*, storm troopers excluded from combat training. The Colonel, however, was doubtful of the military effectiveness of this arrangement; and recommended that an army infantry regiment should be substituted for the SA contingent. His proposal led to the inclusion of 16th Infantry Regiment in air-landing operations in the Sudetenland. Even so, the storm troopers were accepted for training and formed into a separate contingent.

Bassenge, who was in charge of training as well as the operational command of airborne units, now considered his responsibilities as being too onerous for one man alone. Accordingly on 1st July 1938, field command of the force was vested in a new appointment taken up by *Generalmajor* Kurt Student, who at the time was Inspector General of Luftwaffe schools.

The conglomeration of units taken over by General Student consisted of two parachute battalions (*Oberst* Bräuer and *Oberst* Heidrich), a battalion from the Hermann Göring Regiment (*Oberst* Sydow), 16th Infantry Regiment (*Oberst* Kreysing), the contingent from the SA *Regiment Feldherrnhalle*, together with ancillary artillery and medical units. A small glider unit, comprising twelve DFS 230 gliders (*Leutnant* Kiess) and a force of 250 Ju 52 planes (*Oberst* Morzik), were available to transport the assortment of units. Student and his staff aimed at developing these units into a parachute 'light' division, but at first they were by no means certain what they meant by this enterprising idea.

By September 1938 General Student had formally established a somewhat improvised 7th Air Division, which was alerted for air-landing operations at Freudenthal in the Moravian province of Czechoslovakia. But the Czechs conceded the Sudetenland without a fight and the follow-up operation was cancelled. Nevertheless, on 7th October 1938 elements of both the 7th and 22nd (Air-Landing) Divisions were flown into Freudenthal on exercise and many of the transport planes made successful landings on open fields near their objectives. Göring personally witnessed this exercise and was much impressed. Subsequently the units were withdrawn to Germany and dispersed. Infantry Regiment 16 went back to its parent division, 22nd Infantry (Air-Landing) Division, whilst the SA contingent reverted to its former political rôle.

Student was now appointed Inspector of Parachute Troops at the Air Ministry with responsibility also for the technical development of this new arm. During the next seven years Student was to contribute more than any other to the leadership, organisation and military effectiveness of German airborne forces.

The rôle of airborne troops as foreseen in those early days by *Oberst* Bassenge lay in their capacity for surprise and in the speed with which

Germany 1939, for
the first time
parachute troops take
part in the Berlin
military parade.
Adolf Hitler,
Chancellor of the
Third Reich takes the
salute.

they could strike at targets beyond the immediate reach of ground
troops. Key bridges, airfields, communication and supply centres
situated in the enemy's rear were obvious targets to be held in support
of advancing ground forces. But General Student foresaw that the rôle
of airborne troops went far beyond their employment as air-transported
commandos and demolition teams committed to the tactical support of
an army formation. It was as an independent force that Student envisaged the true status of airborne forces: lifted by its own transport;
supported by highly trained and well-equipped ancillary services,
including specialists such as engineers, gunners and signallers; a concept
that in the fullness of time he would demonstrate with the invasion of
Crete.

By the end of 1938 command of all parachute forces had been
transferred to the Luftwaffe. Hitler, who took a personal interest in
airborne developments, ordered that the Luftwaffe should command all
airborne operations until contact was established between airborne and
ground units. This edict did much to clarify command arrangements
and responsibilities until then divided between army and air force
officers.

The army surrendered its parachutists to the air force in the interests
of unified progress and *Major* Heidrich's battalion joined FJR 1 as its
second battalion. The General Staff of the army however maintained its

68

interest in air transportation and experimented with 16th Infantry Regiment and 22nd Infantry Division. The other regiments of the Division, the 47th and 65th Regiments, were not however intensively trained in air-landing methods until early 1940.

With only a few exceptions airborne operations undertaken during the period 1939-1945 were the responsibility of the Luftwaffe, often without reference to the army in planning or assistance in execution. Although SS interest in the airborne idea lay largely dormant, later in the war this service raised several 'special' units that, along with the Abwehr's operations, claim attention for daring and imaginative airborne raids.

The Brandenburg Regiment zbV – *zur besonderen Verwendung*, for special purposes – raised in 1939, was trained in commando raiding methods and included a glider contingent. The regiment, largely recruited from foreign nationals, was employed in the war by army counter intelligence – *Abwehr II* – on sabotage work and later in regimental strength in the rôle of infantry against partisan groups in South East Europe. Expansion to 'divisonal' strength and ultimately conversion into a standard *Panzergrenadier* division took the Brandenburgers to the Eastern front in December 1944. However, control of the parachute battalion had already passed to the SS when, following the attempt on Hitler's life at Rastenburg in July 1944, the SS inherited *Abwehr II* security and intelligence duties.

A further result of this shake-up was the raising of a special SS *Jagdverband* during October 1944 under the command of SS *Obersturmbannführer* Otto Skorzeny. This unit included the SS *Fallschirmjäger-Batallion 500* which performed the sabotage and counter-insurgency duties of the kind associated with the Brandenburg 'Division'. None of these 'special' units ever formed part of the Luftwaffe establishment and their activities only occasionally came within the operational ambit of the airborne corps. Volunteers were invited from the Brandenburg Division by Skorzeny for the *Jagdverband* but few Brandenburgers actually transferred into the SS.

In September 1939, 7th Air Division was established in the North West German garrison towns of Braunschweig, Hildesheim, Gardelegen and Tangermünde under their commander (now) *Generalleutnant* Student. Already, with a few preliminary engagements behind them, German airborne troops – known in Germany as *Luftlandetruppen* – were firmly established as the youngest branch of the armed services. They were trained and equipped as a fighting formation with unrivalled potential anywhere in the world. At Freudenthal in 1938 ideas had become reality and in air-landing exercises at Luneberg in July 1939 this spearhead of the German lance was finally forged. In the same year *Fallschirmjäger* under Colonel Bräuer took part in the great Berlin military parade, their first official presentation to the German public.

Events seemingly augured well for the new arm of the services but when in June General (later Field-Marshal) von Brauchitsch witnessed a specially arranged demonstration at Munsterlage he remained unconvinced of the potential value of air-landing operations. The General commented:

'This is still in its infancy and in the context of tactical employment only a drop in the ocean. If you (Student) expect anything more, then you are indeed a great optimist.'

The General's conservative attitude reflected the opinion of many members of the German General Staff but the parachutists found at least one friend in von Kluge who welcomed the innovation. It was he who as officer commanding the Hanover area promoted the air-landing experiments with Infantry Regiment 16.

A decision was now taken to add a third battalion to the existing two battalions. Plans were discussed for establishing two more regiments, FJR 2 and FJR 3: each regiment consisted of three battalions and divisional medical, anti-tank, reconnaissance and signals detachments. About this time (now) *Generalmajor* Bassenge, divisional chief-of-staff, was transferred from the division to employment as Air Commander, Vienna. The division was thus still in process of being formed when Hitler launched his invasion of Poland on 1st September 1939.

In Poland, 7th Air Division was deployed in Lower Silesia on stand-by to exploit any air-landing opportunities that the Polish campaign might present. 16th Infantry Regiment was committed independently in the rôle of infantry reinforcement north of Lodz. Plans to secure bridges ahead of advancing armoured forces, block river crossings and isolate Polish reserves west of Warsaw were rendered unnecessary by the rapid debacle of the Polish army.

7 Military Operations — Airborne Assault

The invasions of Denmark and Norway were launched simultaneously on 9th April 1940. Units of 1st Parachute Regiment (FJR 1) were committed in company strength in Denmark at Aalborg and Vordingborg in minor but decisive actions to secure strategically important bridges and airfields. Denmark fell on the same day, almost without bloodshed.

Bad weather on 9th April prevented a projected attack by parachutists from FJR 1 on Oslo airfield, but the city later fell to air-transported units. These units were also employed against Stavanger on the west coast of Norway and at Dombas in central Norway. At Dombas in mid-April the German troops were involved in a four-day engagement with Norwegian troops, who were fighting to link up with the British forces that had landed at Andalsnes. The parachutists were obliged to surrender when new supplies of ammunition were delayed by adverse weather conditions. In the northern battle for Narvik in May parachutists of the 1st Battalion were assigned to the army as reinforcements for General Dietl, and they remained in Narvik for a time after the Allied evacuation of Norway on 9th June.

When Hitler turned his attentions to the Low Countries on 10th May the 7th Air Division was to be thoroughly tested for the first time. Key bridges, airfields and fortifications in Belgium and Holland were to be seized by units operating in battalion and company strength. Capture of these objectives was vital to the successful advance of Army Groups A and B across the Belgian and Dutch frontiers. The idea was largely Hitler's own but the operational plan was shaped and carried out by General Student. Some 4,500 trained parachutists were ready for action: the bulk of them supplemented by an air transported division, the 22nd Infantry Division with 12,000 men, would be committed against Holland. Infinitely smaller numbers would be sent against Belgium, their diminutive strength offset by scattering paratroop dummies – *Fallschirmpuppen* – across the country, a ruse that successfully confused the defence and deceived them into believing that the numbers employed against them were much greater than they actually were.

Before first light on 10th May, the first day of Operation 'Yellow', *Fall Gelb*, a mixed force of gliderborne and parachute troops from *Sturmabteilung* (Assault Group) Koch set course from their operational base at Cologne-Wahn for the Belgian frontier fortress at Eban-Emael. Simultaneously, three adjacent bridges spanning the Albert Canal were attacked.

Eban-Emael stood at the northern end of the Liège fortress system.

Its machine-guns covered the adjacent crossings of the Albert Canal, including the nearest bridge at Canne. Artillery batteries covered the roads leading westwards from Maastricht, and the key bridges a little further north at Vroenhoven and Veldwezelt. *Hauptmann* Koch's objectives were the capture of the fortress as well as the three neighbouring bridges.

The modern fortress of Eban-Emael had only recently been built. Six outer walls of reinforced concrete enclosed an area some 1,000 yards long from north to south by 800 yards wide. The longest wall towered 130 feet above the canal itself; and the other walls concealed flood gates and were protected by out-post trenches and wire. In addition to the machine-guns and field artillery, quick-firing cannon, anti-aircraft guns and searchlights were positioned inside the walls. The garrison establishment of about 1,000 infantrymen and gunners possessed stocks of food and water for two months.

'Assault Group Koch', formed by Captain Koch at Hildesheim in November 1939, consisted of his single company of paratroopers (1st Company FJR 1) and the parachute engineer platoon, *Fallschirm-Pioneerzug*, under *Oberleutnant* Witzig. The bridges were not thought to present a problem and these were assigned to Koch's Company split into three sections. Veldwezelt, Vroenhoven and Canne were allocated to Assault Parties Steel (Altmann), Concrete (Schacht) and Iron (Schächter). Whilst these parties were to be parachuted in, a DFS 230 glider contingent carrying the engineer demolitions party (Granite) was to land inside the walls of the fortress. Forty-two Ju 52's were allotted to the task of towing gliders and dropping paratroopers. The glider pilots themselves were actually under the command of *Oberleutnant* Kiess.

On the road to Waalhaven, parachutists and air-landed infantry of Infantry Regiment 16 prepare to move against the town centre.

Holland 1940. A
Ju 52 delivers men
and supplies to
strengthen units of
1st Parachute
Regiment already in
action on the ground.

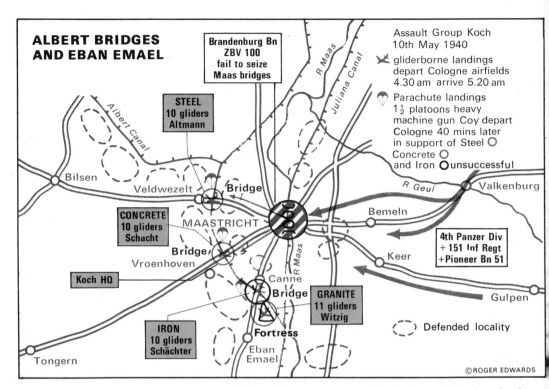

The eleven DFS 230 gliders were towed in darkness into the air above Cologne on the morning of 10th May. The gliders were released before crossing the German frontier and all but four of them sailed successfully across the narrow strip of Holland and landed thirty-five minutes later amongst the sleeping Belgian garrison at Eban-Emael. Two gliders crash-landed *en route* and two chose to land on the wrong targets. During that day the bridges at Veldwezelt and Vroenhoven were taken intact but the Belgian engineers got to Canne first and blew it up in the face of the assault party.

Inside the fortress Witzig's fifty-five engineers debouched from the seven gliders and blew in the exits of the fortress and destroyed two 120 mm. cannon and nine 75 mm. guns with their explosive charges before the Belgian soldiers surrendered. Altogether fourteen guns were destroyed with new hollow charges (*Hohlladungen*) used operationally for the first time. *Oberleutnant* Witzig's party was now trapped with some 700 Belgians but a strong German 'relief' force arrived at dawn the following day. By the brilliant stratagem at Eban-Emael, 'Storm Group Koch', trained in great secrecy and assigned with boldness and determination, greatly accelerated the entry of the German Army Group A into the Low Countries.

In Holland the strategic intention of the German General Staff was to swiftly paralyze resistance and disrupt the movement of Dutch reserves by seizing The Hague, Rotterdam and a few other vital communications centres. Both 7th Air Division and 22nd (Air-landing)

Division were committed on 10th May within the operational framework of an *ad hoc* Air-Landing Corps under General Student. In the south Student would also personally lead the 7th Air Division from Headquarters landed at Waalhaven airport, later to be established near Dordrecht in South Holland, while to the north Graf von Sponeck, commander of 22nd Infantry Division – with the assistance of FJR 2, who would first capture the landing places for them – would lead the air-landed infantry, which comprised IR 47 and IR 65. (The third regiment of the division, IR 16, was placed under command of 7th Air Division.) The 22nd Infantry Division was additionally ordered to seize the Dutch government offices at The Hague and – on personal instructions from the Führer – arrest the Royal Family.

Parachute troops employed in both north (FJR 2) and south (FJR 1) would seize airfields adjacent to The Hague, Rotterdam and Dordrecht and the bridge spanning the Waal at Dordrecht and cross the bridge at Moerdijk on the Maas estuary in the south of the operational area. The bridge at Moerdijk lay on the path of the German Eighteenth Army. After landing at Waalhaven IR 16, placed under the Air Division, was to capture bridges over the Lek (Rhine) near Rotterdam and key positions at Dordrecht; their purpose being to establish a corridor for the 9th Panzer Division after crossing the Maas.

Whilst FJR 2 struggled in the north to capture the airfields vital to the success of the air-landing division, IR 16 disembarked from Ju 52's at Rotterdam's Waalhaven airport, captured by the third battalion of FJR 1. Quickly they pushed forward into the centre of the great Dutch port where they seized an important bridge, seriously blocking the movement of Dutch reinforcements rushing to the area; but it was only after a tragic misunderstanding, resulting in the bombing of the city that the defenders surrendered their positions after four days of fighting. The Moerdijk and Dordrecht bridges were seized by 2nd Battalion/FJR 1, personally led by *Oberst* Bräuer, their regimental commander.

On airfields adjacent to The Hague, at Loosduinen, Ypenburg, Delft and Valkenburg units of FJR 2 fought to reach and establish bridgeheads through which the second wave air-transported battalions of 22nd Infantry Division could assault The Hague. Unhappily for them, many of the paratroopers from FJR 2, dropped in these areas with the intention of opening the way for the Ju 52's, were landed off target and units of IR 47 and IR 65 found themselves landing on unsecured airfields swept by heavy artillery fire. Many planes were indeed obliged to put down on neighbouring highways; an expediency, but wrongly interpreted by Allied military staffs as being part of the tactical plan. The approaches to The Hague were only secured after heavy losses had been sustained by the air transport groups and air-landing infantry; the Dutch government and Royal Family escaped aboard two British destroyers.

Four days after 580 Ju 52 transport planes had crossed the Dutch frontiers; it was almost all over. The Dutch troops had fought bravely, but in spite of French intervention in the south there was no hope of effective help from the Allies. The Allies themselves learned few lessons from the German campaign in Holland. The almost total lack of

Belgium 1940, the victors of Eban Emael. They were later commended by Hitler for their resounding success in wresting control of the strongest fortress in Europe from a garrison nearly one thousand strong.

appreciation of tactical methods and strengths of German airborne forces that persisted in Allied circles contributed in no small measure to the defeat of the garrison in Crete in 1941.

In Britain at the time of the invasion of the Low Countries misapprehension was clearly evidenced in newspaper and radio reports concerning enemy airborne troops. Their rôle and tactics being so little understood, rumour gave rise to many false ideas.

One eye-witness in a widely circulated account published immediately after the fall of Holland and subtitled 'I Saw Them Drop', writes

Transport planes were landing on every beach, every football ground, every open space and were pouring out troops. A great majority of them were disguised – as civilians, as Dutch soldiers, as policemen and railwaymen. Thousands of Dutchmen, hailing them as comrades, were losing their lives at the hands of these men, who have been ordered to stop at nothing.

Other reports said that parachutists were dropped in large numbers disguised as nuns and might be expected to function more as 'fifth columnists' than conventional soldiers. They were expected to carry street maps marked with the names and addresses of Nazi sympathisers. Consequently, elaborate precautions were taken to render farm land and open spaces throughout Britain unsuitable for landing operations by transport planes and gliders.

Further measures included the raising of Local Defence Volunteers, ill-armed but enthusiastic civilians, who were to keep a watchful eye on their local football ground and neighbouring places where parachute landings might be effected. The LDV were later embodied into a Home Guard whose duties included the protection of factories, petrol stations, airfields and other targets that might attract the attention of enemy sabotage agents.

The invasion of Britain was of course part of Hitler's master plan. Borne triumphantly on the tide of success in Poland in the East and in Denmark, Norway, the Low Countries and France in the West, on 2nd July 1940 Hitler ordered preliminary staff studies for Operation 'Sealion'. In early August the Army Supreme Command, *Oberkommando des Heeres* or OKH, discussed plans for the use of 7th Air Division in forming bridgeheads on the South coast of Britain, with assistance from von Runstedt's Ninth and Sixteenth Armies. Changes in the original plan required 7th Air Division to establish forward positions on the South Downs and northwards from Dover. The Luftwaffe raised technical objections however and it was finally decided that parachutists should be employed to secure a crossing of the Royal Military Canal, which extends across the Romney Marsh from Kent into Sussex, and hold off any attack mounted against Sixteenth Army from a northwesterly direction. They would then be available also to assist the Sixteenth Army's advance from beaches on the South coast between Worthing and Folkestone to Dover. The cliffs at Dover were also to be seized by parachutists.

The 22nd (Air-Landing) Division was intended for use in the first wave of Sixteenth Army's assault from across the channel. Fortunately for Britain and thanks to the Royal Air Force, the Luftwaffe did not secure air superiority over Southern England and the German Navy was lacking in the necessary confidence to mount and sustain the projected invasion. Operation 'Sealion' was deferred on 12th October; as it turned out, indefinitely,

The success of the airborne troops and their immense contribution to German victory in the West was clearly evident; their unique capacity for speed and surprise amply demonstrated. In consequence of their proven ability completion of the full establishment of the 7th Air

ORGANISATION OF THE AD HOC AIR-LANDING CORPS FOR THE ATTACK ON HOLLAND

10th May 1940

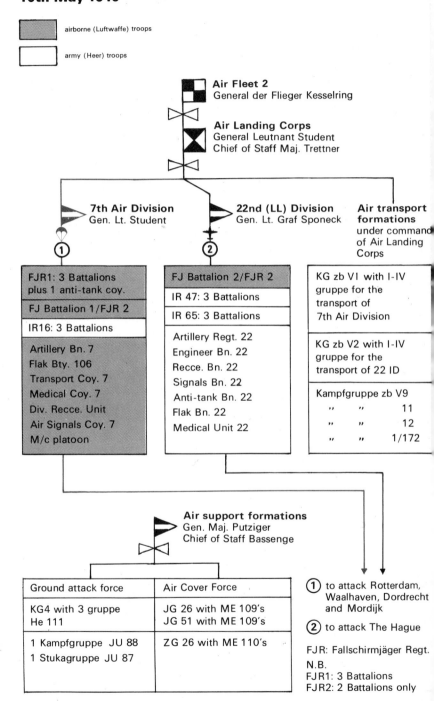

airborne (Luftwaffe) troops

army (Heer) troops

Air Fleet 2
General der Flieger Kesselring

Air Landing Corps
General Leutnant Student
Chief of Staff Maj. Trettner

7th Air Division
Gen. Lt. Student

22nd (LL) Division
Gen. Lt. Graf Sponeck

Air transport formations
under command of Air Landing Corps

① FJR1: 3 Battalions plus 1 anti-tank coy.

FJ Battalion 1/FJR 2

IR16: 3 Battalions

Artillery Bn. 7
Flak Bty. 106
Transport Coy. 7
Medical Coy. 7
Div. Recce. Unit
Air Signals Coy. 7
M/c platoon

② FJ Battalion 2/FJR 2

IR 47: 3 Battalions

IR 65: 3 Battalions

Artillery Regt. 22
Engineer Bn. 22
Recce. Bn. 22
Signals Bn. 22
Anti-tank Bn. 22
Flak Bn. 22
Medical Unit 22

KG zb VI with I-IV gruppe for the transport of 7th Air Division

KG zb V2 with I-IV gruppe for the transport of 22 ID

Kampfgruppe zb V9
" " 11
" " 12
" " 1/172

Air support formations
Gen. Maj. Putziger
Chief of Staff Bassenge

Ground attack force	Air Cover Force
KG4 with 3 gruppe He 111	JG 26 with ME 109's JG 51 with ME 109's
1 Kampfgruppe JU 88 1 Stukagruppe JU 87	ZG 26 with ME 110's

① to attack Rotterdam, Waalhaven, Dordrecht and Mordijk

② to attack The Hague

FJR: Fallschirmjäger Regt.

N.B.
FJR1: 3 Battalions
FJR2: 2 Battalions only

78

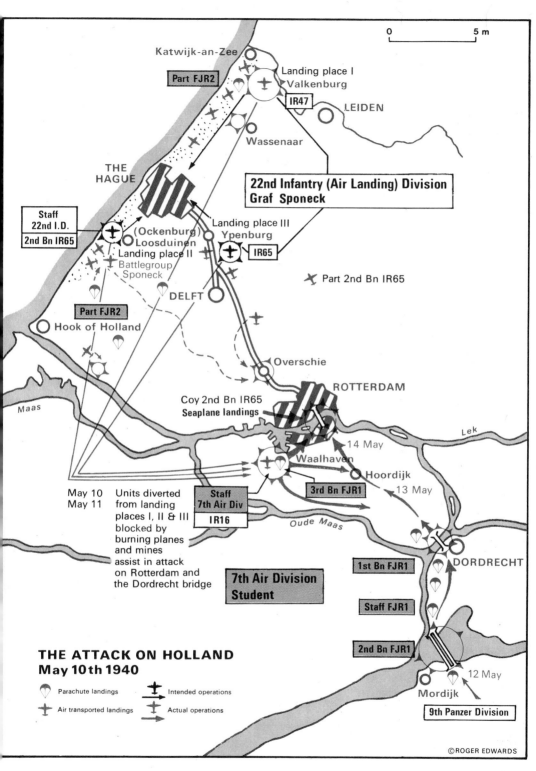

Katwijk-an-Zee

Part FJR2

Landing place I
Valkenburg

IR47

LEIDEN

Wassenaar

THE HAGUE

22nd Infantry (Air Landing) Division Graf Sponeck

Staff 22nd I.D.
2nd Bn IR65

(Ockenburg)
Loosduinen
Landing place II
Battlegroup
Sponeck

Landing place III
Ypenburg

IR65

✈ Part 2nd Bn IR65

DELFT

Part FJR2

○ Hook of Holland

Overschie

ROTTERDAM

Maas

Coy 2nd Bn IR65
Seaplane landings

Waalhaven

14 May

Hoordijk

Lek

May 10   Units diverted
May 11   from landing
          places I, II & III
          blocked by
          burning planes
          and mines
          assist in attack
          on Rotterdam and
          the Dordrecht bridge

Staff 7th Air Div
IR16

3rd Bn FJR1

13 May

Oude Maas

7th Air Division Student

1st Bn FJR1

DORDRECHT

Staff FJR1

2nd Bn FJR1

12 May

THE ATTACK ON HOLLAND
May 10th 1940

Mordijk

9th Panzer Division

◗ Parachute landings   ✈ Intended operations

✚ Air transported landings ➤ Actual operations

©ROGER EDWARDS

0   5 m

79

Division was accelerated; losses made good and setbacks overcome with maximum efficiency. One setback experienced by the division was caused by the temporary incapacitation of General Student, who was hit in the head by a stray bullet at Rotterdam in Holland. General Putziger was appointed to the temporary command of the division and later General Süssmann.

The gliderborne contingents of Assault Group Koch which had performed so well at Eban-Emael were expanded into 1st Battalion/1st Assault Regiment. Personnel for 7th Air Division were recruited from other Luftwaffe units and also from the army. More significantly for the success of future operations, air transport groups were allotted to the division as a separate formation. Close co-operation in training was thus assured. *Generalmajor* Gerhard Conrad who commanded the new formation, was as a Colonel awarded the Knight's Cross for his exploits with airborne troops in the Low Countries.

With rapidly increasing problems of co-ordination and control, the airborne divisions and their support formations were officially raised to Corps status. XI Air Corps was formally established in summer 1940 and General Student was promoted to (Air) General, and named as Air Officer Commanding the new corps.

The opportunity for the useful employment of XI Corps was soon to arise in Greece. The British Imperial forces, after first landing in Greece in March 1941 in the hope of bolstering the gallant but inadequately equipped and now largely immobile army of King George II, were withdrawing southwards from their original positions west of the Vardar river under pressure from armoured elements of the German Twelfth Army. Across their path into the Southern Peloponnese lay the narrow strip of land cut by the Corinth canal. A single bridge provided a crossing over the canal.

The task of securing this bridge intact in advance of Twelfth Army was assigned to the reinforced 2nd Parachute Regiment (FJR 2) under *Oberst* Sturm. FJR 2 had in March been moved into Bulgaria prior to forestalling a possible British occupation of Lemnos. Instead the Aegean island was occupied by other German units, so the need for the operation did not arise. With the Twelfth Army now racing through Greece, Sturm's regiment was given the vital task of capturing the Corinth bridge.

Oberst Sturm's plan was to attack the bridge with a battle group of fifty-two parachute engineers (*Fallschirmpioniere*) supported by the 1st and 2nd Battalions of FJR 2, together with signals and medical detachments. The engineers were commanded by *Leutnant* Häffner *Hauptmann* Kroh's 1st Battalion was to land north of the bridge and *Hauptmann* Pietzonka's 2nd Battalion to the south.

The assembly area and point of departure for the operation was the Greek airfield at Larissa. The force of 270 Ju 52's under *Oberst* von Heyking took off at 0500 hours on the morning of 25th April 1941. The bridge lay two hours flying time from the airfield. The gliders landed promptly at 0700 hours and Häffner's engineers seized the bridge after exchanging fire with the defenders. The engineers were now strongly counter-attacked and the situation was not relieved until the late arrival of Pietzonka's battalion from the south.

The purpose of the attack was of course to secure the Corinth bridge intact. In spite of the heavy fighting that ensued on both sides of the bridge, Sturm's plan looked as if it was succeeding until a British shell hit the bridge. Although British demolition charges had been removed by the German engineers, no reason has ever been given as to why the bridge collapsed under the impact of possibly a stray shell. German losses were slight. Eight only of the engineers were killed; *Leutnant* Häffner surviving only to be drowned less than a month later on board the First Light Ship Flotilla bound for Crete.

A temporary structure was erected and on the morning of 28th April advance guards of Twelfth Army crossed the canal in pursuit of the Allied troops now embarking from harbours further south in the Peloponnese. The evacuation by the Royal Navy was completed by 29th April, although the Germans were successful in cutting off certain detachments at Nauplia and Kalimata. Of 43,000 troops taken off from Greek ports by the Royal Navy, 27,000 were landed in Crete. But for the lone shell at Corinth a considerable number of these men would not have escaped from Greece; and the rather fortuitous opportunity to reinforce the garrison on Crete would not have arisen.

With the successful invasion of the Balkans and much of South East Europe falling into German hands, contingency plans for assaults on Malta and Crete were discussed by the Armed Services High Command *Oberkommando der Wehrmacht* or OKW. Anxiety persisted over the need to prevent the Royal Air Force from using the islands as bases for raids on the Rumanian oilfields, and Germany's newly extended southern flank in South East Europe.

Although preoccupied with planning the imminent invasion of Russia (Operation 'Barbarossa'), Field-Marshal Keitel, Head of OKW and General Jodl, his Chief of Operations, listened attentively to General Student's plan to capture Crete. This plan had been presented to Göring on 5th April by General Löhr, GOC Fourth Air Fleet. Göring thought highly of the plan. But OKW were more concerned by the greater threat posed to their North African strategy by the British fleet based at Malta. Student argued that Crete was the more suitable for an assault by XI Air Corps. Hitler, to whom the plan was submitted on 21st April, the day on which the Greek army on Epirus capitulated to Field-Marshal List, was in a receptive mood but doubted its practicability. Nevertheless he promised to study the project in the context of Axis grand strategy.

On 25th April, Hitler with some misgivings gave his approval to the Cretan plan and issued Directive 28 'an operation to occupy the island of Crete (Operation 'Mercury'), to be prepared with the object of using Crete as an air base against Britain in the Eastern Mediterranean.' The operation was to be exclusively an air force affair with executive responsibility in the hands of General Löhr. Göring gave his full support to the plan, seeing in it the Luftwaffe's opportunity to win the laurels so emphatically denied to him in the Battle of Britain.

The mounting of Operation 'Mercury' called for the resources of the full establishment of XI Air Corps. The airborne corps, 7th Air

Division, with 5th Mountain Division seconded from Twelfth Army in place of 22nd (Air-Landing) Division, were duly assembled in the neighbourhood of Athens in Southern Greece under the command of Air-General Student, GOC XI Air Corps. The weapons and equipment belonging to 7th Air Division were lying packed in the containers assembled in Northern France for Operation 'Sealion'. The containers were transported by rail to the Black Sea port of Constanza, thence shipped to the Corps assembly area around Athens. Personnel of the division were moved in from German garrison towns by rail and road.

Responsibility for bomber and fighter support was given to VIII Air Corps under the command of *Generalleutnant* Freiherr von Richthofen. The backbone of the group were the Ju 87 dive-bomber squadrons, numbering some 150 machines. Support for them was provided by three groups of Do 17 bombers, Ju 88's and six fighter groups operating Me 109's and Me 110's.

Ten air transport groups of KGzbV 1, 2 and 3, attached to XI Air Corps, mustering roughly 500 Ju 52's, and three glider towing groups of LLG 1 were under the command of *Generalmajor* Conrad. The transport planes and gliders of these groups were responsible for lifting the parachute and mountain troops assembled at departure airfields at Tanágra, Topolis, Dadion, Mégara, Corinth, Phaleron and Elevsis. All these airfields lay within a distance of 80 miles from Athens. The Ju 87 Stuka squadrons were scheduled to operate from Elevsis, Phaleron and the island of Scarpanto (now Karpathos). This latter airfield lay only a few minutes flying time across the Kasos Strait from Crete. Athens was selected as XI Air Corps battle headquarters.

By storming the Metaxas Line covering the Bulgarian frontier, Ringel's 5th Mountain Division had already contributed distinguished services to Field-Marshal List's Twelfth Army in Greece. Still in Northern Greece the mountain troops were selected to replace 22nd Air-Landing Division as partner to 7th Air Division. A strenuous march brought the mountain troops to their assembly point near Athens where, after a three-week period of intensive training, the division achieved a reasonable state of readiness for the coming battle.

The 22nd Division, the 7th's former partner in Holland, was employed at the time on oilfield protection duties at Ploesti; hindered in Rumania by the inadequacies of the road system. The problem of the roads and priority troop movements in the opposite direction for Operation 'Barbarossa' weighed heavily against the chances of rapidly moving the division to the Greek airfields. In consequence the more conveniently situated mountain division was brought into the plan.

Operation 'Mercury' was scheduled for 20th May. XI Air Corps' operational plan called for airborne landings in four places on the mountainous island of Crete which is 160 miles long by 40 miles broad. Due to inadequate air transport facilities the plan was of necessity phased into two airborne assault waves (paratroops) and an air-landing wave (mountain troops). The same transports, after their return to the departure airfields, would re-assemble and be used for the later air lifts. Máleme and Canea were the objectives for the first lift (morning), Retimo and Herakleion for the second (afternoon), while all three

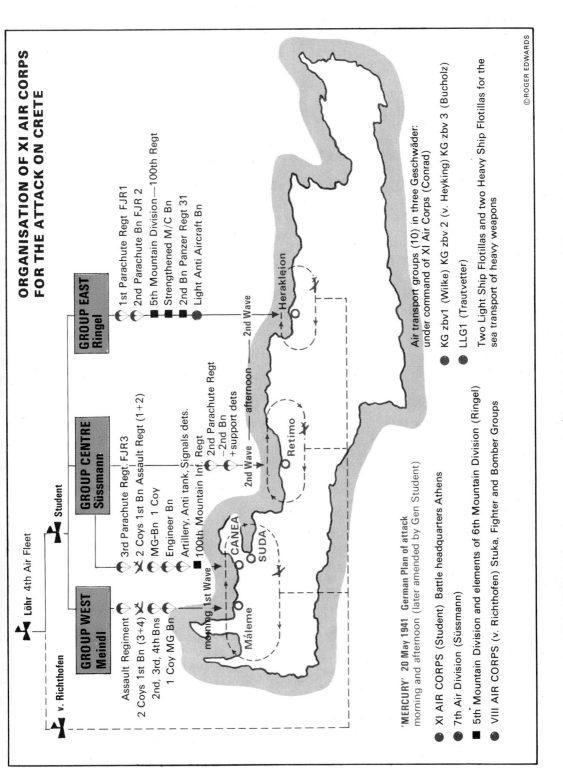

ORGANISATION OF XI AIR CORPS FOR THE ATTACK ON CRETE

Löhr 4th Air Fleet

v. Richthofen

Student

GROUP WEST Meindl

Assault Regiment
2 Coys 1st Bn (3+4)
2nd, 3rd, 4th Bns
1 Coy MG Bn

GROUP CENTRE Süssmann

3rd Parachute Regt. FJR3
2 Coys 1st Bn Assault Regt (1+2)
MG-Bn 1 Coy
Engineer Bn
Artillery, Anti tank, Signals dets.
100th Mountain Inf. Regt
2nd Parachute Regt
— 2nd Bn
+ support dets

GROUP EAST Ringel

1st Parachute Regt FJR1
2nd Parachute Bn FJR 2
5th Mountain Division—100th Regt
Strengthened M/C Bn
2nd Bn Panzer Regt 31
Light Anti Aircraft Bn

Máleme

CANEA

SUDA

morning 1st Wave

Retimo

2nd Wave — afternoon

Herakleion

2nd Wave

2nd Wave — afternoon

Air transport groups (10) in three Geschwäder:
under command of XI Air Corps (Conrad)

KG zbv1 (Wilke) KG zbv 2 (v. Heyking) KG zbv 3 (Bucholz)

LLG1 (Trautvetter)

Two Light Ship Flotillas and two Heavy Ship Flotillas for the
sea transport of heavy weapons

'MERCURY' 20 May 1941 German Plan of attack
morning and afternoon (later amended by Gen Student)

- XI AIR CORPS (Student) Battle headquarters Athens
- 7th Air Division (Süssmann)
- 5th Mountain Division and elements of 6th Mountain Division (Ringel)
- VIII AIR CORPS (v. Richthofen) Stuka, Fighter and Bomber Groups

©ROGER EDWARDS

landing areas were to be reinforced by the third air lift.

Morning, May 20th: Advance elements of Group West were due to land
first in gliders at 0715 hours on 20th May. The remainder of *Generalmajor* Meindl's assault regiment (three battalions of 1,860 men) were to
capture Máleme aerodrome, situated near the northwestern extremity of
the island. After making contact with detachments of Süssmann's
Group Centre, dropped simultaneously on their left near the naval base
at Suda, the assault regiment's secondary task was to assist in the
capture of the capital at Canea (Khania).

The group's gliderborne element consisted of the 1st (Glider) Battalion Headquarters under *Major* Koch, 3rd Company under *Leutnant*
von Plessen with twelve gliders and 4th Company under *Hauptmann*
Sarrazin with fifteen gliders. Their objectives were the AA positions and
camp south of the airfield. A regimental headquarters battle group in
nine gliders under command of Brigade-Major Braun would attempt to
seize the Tavronitis bridge close to the airfield. *Generalmajor* Süssman,
the 7th Division's commander, and his staff in five gliders were to arrive
with Group Centre, which consisted principally of FJR 3 under *Oberst*
Heidrich. The paratroopers were to be later reinforced by mountain
troops, the combined objectives being the capture of Canea, the capital,
and the towns of Suda and Galatas. Canea is located 25 miles east of
Máleme. The group's secondary task was the capture of Retimo, a
distance of some 25 miles further east along the coast, and was entrusted to FJR 2 and scheduled for the early afternoon. Two gliderborne
companies, 1st Company under Altmann and 2nd Company under
Genz detached from the Assault Regiment, carried in thirty gliders,
were given the special task of neutralizing anti-aircraft positions south
and west of Canea and Suda in a preliminary action fifteen minutes
before the main regimental landing. Altogether a force of roughly 3,000
men was involved.

Afternoon, May 20th: In the afternoon phase of the operation FJR 2,
with a force of 1,500 men under *Oberst* Sturm, would make for the
airport at Retimo. In the same airborne wave Group East, consisting
principally of FJR 1 with 2,600 men under *Oberst* Bräuer (including a
battalion seconded from FJR 2), was to be followed in by
Generalleutnant Ringel's 5th Mountain Division less one regiment
landed from the sea. A tank battalion would follow when it could safely
make the sea crossing from Piraeus. The objectives in this area lay with
the capture of the town and airfield at Herakleion (Candia), which is
situated centrally on the northern coastline of the island. Herakleion
was also hopefully to be taken before nightfall on the first day.

Support weapons, anti-tank and anti-aircraft machine-guns from
corps and divisional specialist units were allotted to each group in
accordance with their expected needs. The parachute engineers were
assigned a special flank protection task for FJR 3 under Group Centre
at Alikianou, a few miles south of Máleme.

Seaborne support for the operation was projected in the shape of two
hastily gathered and improvised flotillas of shallow draught motor-
cutters. Escorted by motor torpedo boats of the Italian navy, they would

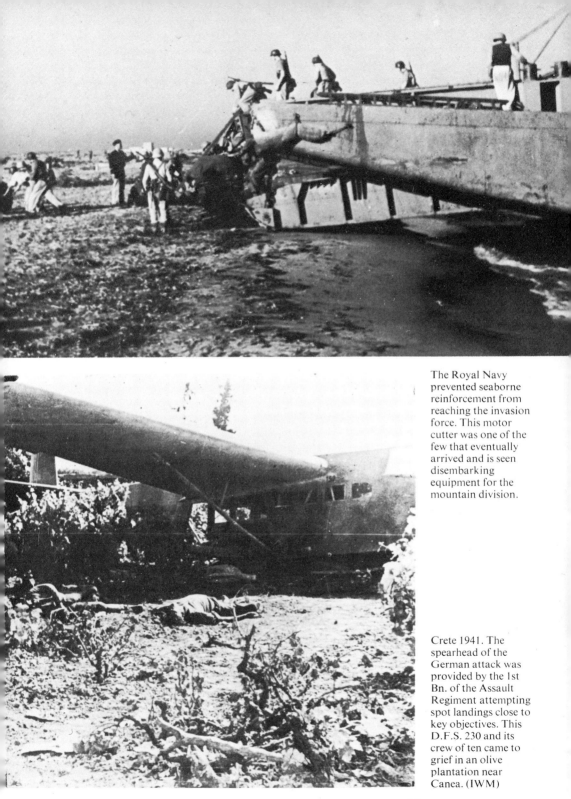

The Royal Navy prevented seaborne reinforcement from reaching the invasion force. This motor cutter was one of the few that eventually arrived and is seen disembarking equipment for the mountain division.

Crete 1941. The spearhead of the German attack was provided by the 1st Bn. of the Assault Regiment attempting spot landings close to key objectives. This D.F.S. 230 and its crew of ten came to grief in an olive plantation near Canea. (IWM)

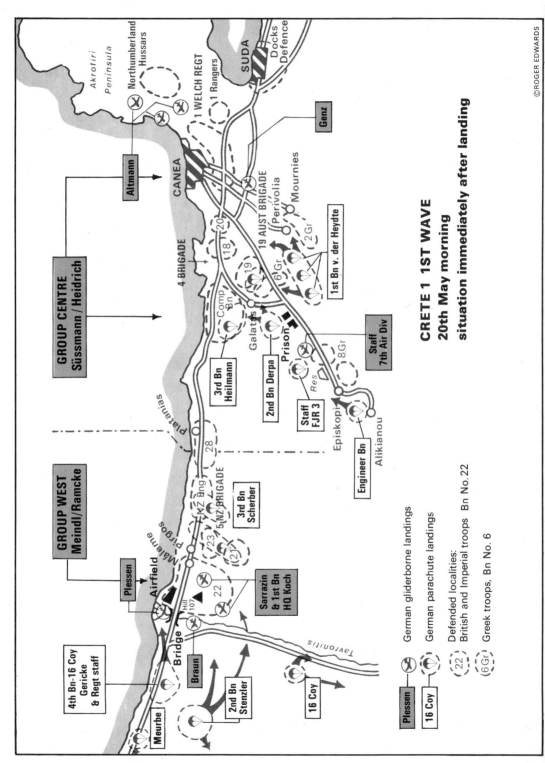

CRETE 1 1ST WAVE
20th May morning
situation immediately after landing

GROUP WEST
Meindl/Ramcke

GROUP CENTRE
Süssmann / Heidrich

Altmann

Genz

Akrotiri Peninsula

Northumberland Hussars

1 WELCH REGT

1 Rangers

SUDA

Docks Defence

CANEA

4 BRIGADE

19 AUST BRIGADE

Mournies

Perivolia

2 Gr

1st Bn v. der Heydte

6 Gr

20

18

19

Comp Bn

Galatas

Prison

3rd Bn Heilmann

2nd Bn Derpa

Staff FJR 3

Res

8 Gr

Staff 7th Air Div

Episkopi

Alikianou

Engineer Bn

Platanias

28

NZ Eng

5 NZ BRIGADE

3rd Bn Scherber

23

21

22

Hill 107

Sarrazin & 1st Bn HQ Koch

Plessen

Airfield

Maleme

Pirgos

Bridge

Braun

Tavronitis

2nd Bn Stenzler

16 Coy

4th Bn-16 Coy Gericke & Regt staff

Meurbe

©ROGER EDWARDS

German gliderborne landings

German parachute landings

Defended localities:
British and Imperial troops Bn No. 22

Greek troops, Bn No. 6

22

6 Gr

Plessen

16 Coy

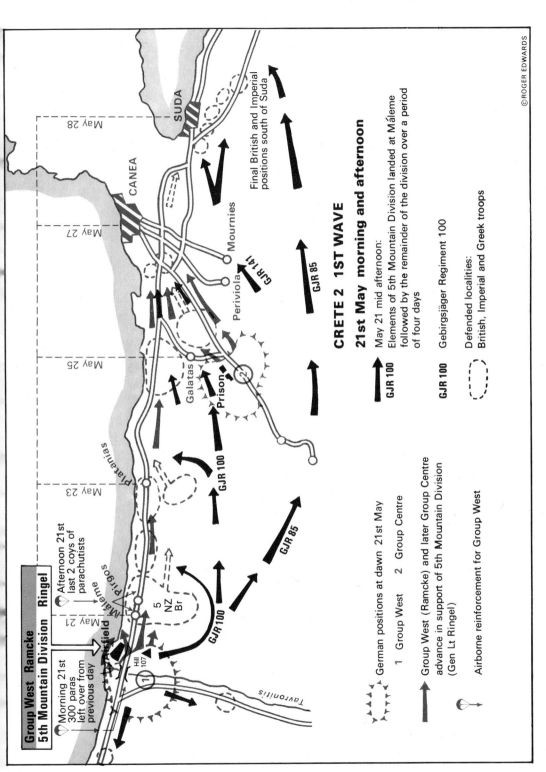

CRETE 2 1ST WAVE
21st May morning and afternoon

Group West Ramcke
5th Mountain Division Ringel

Morning 21st
300 paras
left over from
previous day

Afternoon 21st
last 2 coys of
parachutists

May 21

Maleme

Pirgos

Airfield

Hill
107

1

Tavronitis

5
NZ
Br

Platanias

May 23

May 25

Prison

2

Galatas

Periviola

Mournies

CANEA

May 27

May 28

SUDA

GJR 141

GJR 85

GJR 100

GJR 100

GJR 100

GJR 85

Final British and Imperial
positions south of Suda

May 21 mid afternoon:
Elements of 5th Mountain Division landed at Máleme
followed by the remainder of the division over a period
of four days

GJR 100 Gebirgsjäger Regiment 100

Defended localities:
British, Imperial and Greek troops

German positions at dawn 21st May
1 Group West   2 Group Centre

Group West (Ramcke) and later Group Centre
advance in support of 5th Mountain Division
(Gen Lt Ringel)

Airborne reinforcement for Group West

©ROGER EDWARDS

87

More successful was
the action to capture
the bridge over the
dried up Tavronitis
where four gliders
achieved a near
perfect landing. They
came down in close
formation within a
few hundred yards of
their objective.

The bulk of the
invasion force
parachuted in from
Ju 52s flying from
Greece a distance of
approximately one
hour's flying time from
the island. Casualties
in men and machines
were catastrophic.
(IWM)

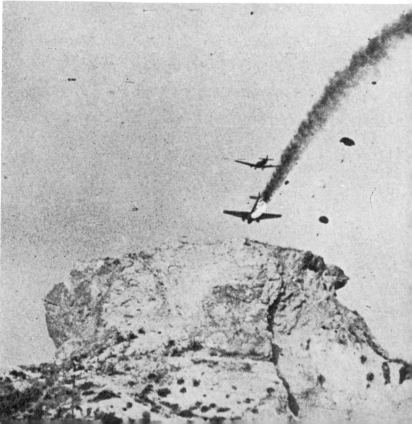

attempt to land two battalions of the mountain division with their
vehicles, anti-aircraft and support weapons, as well as detachments of
parachutists, including engineer and anti-tank units, excluded from the
airborne phase of the operation. Landings would be effected on the
open coast at two points on the north coast of the island. One battalion
in twenty-five boats was destined for Máleme in support of Group West
on the evening of the first day and the other battalion on the second day
in a larger flotilla of thirty-eight vessels was intended for Herakleion in
support of Group East.

In the event the first day did not go according to plan. The Imperial
garrison, consisting of 28,000 troops, was larger and far more effective
than the Germans had anticipated. In addition Greek battalions and
Cretan irregulars were distributed amongst the various sectors. The total
strength was about 42,500 men. None of the first day's objectives was
achieved and by evening only Group West looked capable of eventually
achieving its objective. The battle had opened before the first German
parachutist touched the ground. As the gliders floated loose and massed
waves of paratroopers appeared in the sky, they were greeted by lethal
fire.

Many of Group West had landed westwards out of sight of the
defenders at Máleme; but although their principal objectives, Hill 107
and the airfield, had not been taken, the Group's dispositions were still
moderately well placed to carry out their original plan of attack. But the
battalions of this group, especially the 3rd Battalion of the Assault
Regiment under *Major* Scherber dropped east of Máleme, were almost

Wrecked and burned
out Junkers littered
the northern part of
the island, especially
so at Máleme where
they were eventually
disposed of by a
captured British
bulldozer that cleared
the airfield for the
in-coming transports
of the Mountain
Division.

89

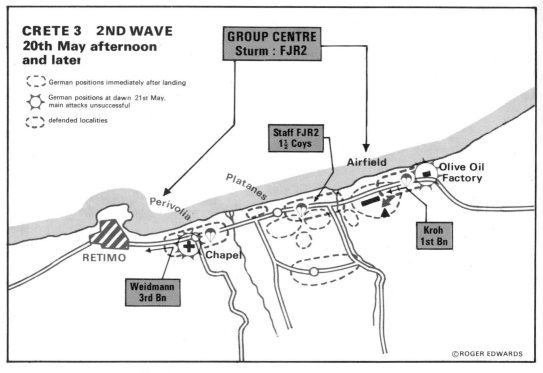

CRETE 3   2ND WAVE
20th May afternoon
and later

⟨ ⟩ German positions immediately after landing

⟨ ⟩ German positions at dawn 21st May,
main attacks unsuccessful

⟨ ⟩ defended localities

GROUP CENTRE
Sturm : FJR2

Staff FJR2
1½ Coys

Airfield

Olive Oil
Factory

Platanes

Perivolia

Kroh
1st Bn

RETIMO

Chapel

Weidmann
3rd Bn

©ROGER EDWARDS

totally destroyed before they reached the ground. Further along the coastline at Retimo and Herakleion the gliderborne and parachute companies of Group Centre and Group East met with such intensive fire from British and Australian troops during the day that their military effectiveness was slight; their losses so great as to virtually put them out of the fight. *Oberst* Heidrich's force dropped in the centre into what was known by the British as 'Prison Valley' south of Galatas, proved the exception to the rule in this area.

On the evening of the first day General Student faced a critical situation at his Headquarters in Athens. All but a small force of his parachutists had been in action during the day and the first flotilla of the seaborne forces intended for Máleme had been delayed and was later to be scattered or sunk on the second day by the Royal Navy. The second flotilla was to fare little better and put back into Milos.

The General's means of getting the upper hand in the battle for Crete were now seemingly limited. 5th Mountain Division, earmarked for the eastern sector of the island, was almost intact but fewer than 600 of his parachutists remained uncommitted. Retimo and Herakleion were still firmly held by the defence. After careful deliberation, later confirmed by reports gathered directly from Máleme by a lone reconnaissance officer, *Hauptmann* Kleye, the General decided to redeploy the 5th Mountain Division to give greater weight to the attack on the New Zealanders there on the following day. Given more strength in consolidation, his new plan, communicated to the attacking regiments on the island at four a. m. was to 'roll-up' Freyberg's defences from the west.

90

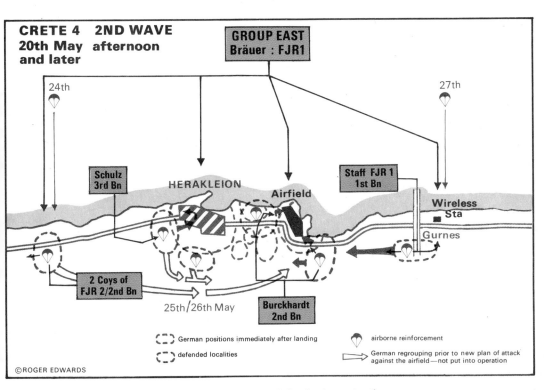

CRETE 4   2ND WAVE
20th May   afternoon
and later

GROUP EAST
Bräuer : FJR1

24th

27th

Schulz
3rd Bn

HERAKLEION

Airfield

Staff FJR 1
1st Bn

Wireless
Sta

Gurnes

2 Coys of
FJR 2/2nd Bn

25th/26th May

Burckhardt
2nd Bn

☐ German positions immediately after landing

☐ defended localities

⛱ airborne reinforcement

⇨ German regrouping prior to new plan of attack
against the airfield—not put into operation

©ROGER EDWARDS

So many difficulties had belaboured the original plan. At the onset
the transports on the makeshift runways in Greece had thrown up
heavy dust clouds. In the confusion the pilots had found it impossible
to make formation and effect properly coordinated approaches to their
dropping zones. Even more chaos reigned as planes were turned round
for successive lifts. Many of the parachutists did not reach their right
locations. Exceptionally heavy losses were sustained by Group Centre;
their objectives in the Canea-Suda area being held by a composite force
of 14,800 men. The capture of the town of Canea and the airfield at
Retimo, held by the 19th Australian Brigade, by nightfall on the first
evening was clearly out of the question.

The two gliderborne companies from the Assault Regiment under
Hauptmann Altmann and *Leutnant* Genz, mounted altogether in some
thirty gliders, achieved a limited degree of success, although many
gliders were destroyed by defensive fire and others smashed up on
landing. A small detachment under *Leutnant* Genz was successful in
capturing the AA guns at Canea; but others failed in their task of
reaching the wireless station; and of those attempting a link-up with
Heidrich fewer than thirty made contact with his force in 'Prison Valley'.

From the moment of leaping from their planes men of Group Centre
suffered badly. Nearly all of the men who came down near Galatas
were killed at once. Many were too widely scattered to form concentrated battle groups. Some companies were spread out over a distance
of nearly three miles and by nightfall the survivors of the drop were still
scattered and ineffective.

Gebirgsjäger of 5th Mountain Division prepare to board a transport. Their coolness and skilful deployment in support of the parachutists saved the invasion from total disaster.

The mountain troops were quick to adapt themselves to the inhospitable terrain. Life jackets were issued for the flight to the island. (IWM)

In 'Prison Valley' the situation was critical. There, Heidrich and the rump of FJR 3, numbering fewer than a thousand fit men, were unable to break out of a cordon of Australian troops for several days. The paratroopers remained in the centre of a welter of fire until a link was forged with troops advancing along the coast from Máleme.

The German schedule had gone badly astray. Surprise had not been achieved. Chaos reigned on the airfields in Greece. Communications between the home base and the troops on the ground were practically non-existent although from the very first moment of the attack a wireless link was established with the Assault Regiment at Máleme. Failures in the timing of flight plans led to delay in arrival of troops in their operational areas. Air formations did not link up in correct tactical sequence and others were landed without fighter protection. This was due largely to inadequate telephone communication between the transport groups and fighter squadrons. The airborne force that had been despatched to Crete was some 600 men short of its operational strength.

Apart from these unexpected mishaps, the failure of the German Intelligence Services was also serious. Assessments of the strength of the garrison were conflicting and the morale and efficiency of the defenders had been underestimated. Geographical features and detail had been wrongly interpreted from air reconnaissance photographs; the result, gliders and men were sent crashing headlong into terraced hillsides whereas comparitively smooth landings had been expected.

At Máleme on the second day the situation showed signs of improvement for the Germans. General Student boldly decided to commit his reserve parachutists; a small force of 550 men remaining at base. Fortune now smiled on Operation 'Mercury'. Imagining their forward companies to be overwhelmed, the remains of two New Zealand brigades began to withdraw from the Máleme area during the course of that night. When fighting patrols from Group West reached Hill 107, a key feature in the defence of the airfield, they were easily able to overcome what little opposition remained.

The vital airfield now lay almost within German grasp. The scratch force of paratroopers was despatched to Máleme in support of Group West; *Generalmajor* Meindl, its wounded commander, had already been flown out and was now replaced by *Oberst* Ramcke, a resolute veteran of the First World War and a comparatively new recruit to the airborne corps. Immediately on arrival Ramcke assumed command of the Group and skilfully proceeded to unlock the 'gateway' to the eastern route along the coast.

Máleme airfield was still under artillery fire when in the late afternoon Student now sent in the first of the redeployed mountain troops, 100 Battalion under *Oberst* Utz, by air. The Ju 52 transports flew their precious cargoes of men and supplies into an inferno of blazing planes and exploding shells. Transport planes were piled up everywhere, even one on top of another. Many of the Junkers were shot to pieces or lay burned out on the beaches. Heavy casualties amongst the mountain riflemen were avoided through the presence of mind of the pilots but losses in planes were extremely heavy.

A unit of 1st Parachute Regiment moving to new positions uses a donkey yoked to a container to minimise fatigue in sweltering heat.

Generalleutnant Student visiting the island for the first time on the 25th May, from his battle headquarters in Athens, receives a report from an orderly at Oberst Ramcke's H.Q. The colonel is standing to the general's left.

In spite of the holocaust the bulk of the mountain battalion, together with a regimental headquarters totalling 650 men, were landed safely. Under Ramcke's command the fighting capacity of Group West was quickly revived. Ramcke was confident of holding his ground at Máleme against an expected counter-attack but the Colonel's confidence was not shared by the far-distant High Command. Hitler and Göring, dismayed at the losses suffered by the parachutists, would allow no mention of the Cretan landing to be made in the press or on the radio.

On the third day, with Máleme in German hands and the awaited counter-attack launched and halted, further battalions of mountain riflemen reached the island, together with their divisional commander, *Generalmajor* Ringel. Süssmann being dead, Ringel now took overall command of the forces on the ground; and over the next five days systematically proceeded to implement General Student's plan of rolling up the defence from the west. After Máleme Canea fell and Student flew in to see what was left of his Corps.

Contact was made with Heidrich and the remnants of Group Centre, a combined force of mountain troops and parachutists, then a major attack was mounted to clear the Canea-Suda area. FJR 2 at Retimo had conceded many prisoners, including their commander, *Oberst* Sturm. The prisoners were freed and with the parachutists in reserve the 5th Mountain Division, augmented by a regiment from 6th Mountain Division, launched the final drive to clear the island of defenders. Suda Bay, Retimo and Herakleion fell in quick succession.

By 24th May, General Freyberg had abandoned hope of holding Crete, and, in view of the heavy losses being suffered by the Royal Navy, the decision to evacuate the island was made on 27th May. The following day the majority of the defence forces broke off the engagement and retreated to the southern port of Sphakia (Chora Sphakion). As dawn broke on the 27th Laycock's Commandos were holding a defensive position astride the main road inland from Sphakia. Unmercifully dive-bombed by Stukas, Captain Evelyn Waugh, the novelist, who was present observed that 'Like all things German it is very efficient, but it goes on much too long.'

Severe losses were sustained in attempts by the Royal Navy to embark troops from the northern parts of the island, although a successful evacuation was made at Herakleion. At Retimo Ringel's mountain troops and an armoured battalion with tanks and motor cycles now landed from the sea enforced large-scale surrender, but some of the defenders escaped to the mountains and fought on as partisan groups. The last evacuation was made from a beach at Sphakia on 31st May.

Allied casualties in the campaign were about 17,500 killed, wounded and prisoners. 12,000 British, Australian and New Zealand troops went into captivity, but the number of Greek soldiers and Cretan fighters taken was never precisely known. In addition nine British warships were sunk, and seventeen were damaged. Rather more than half of the total garrison of 42,500 men were carried by the Royal Navy across the Mediterranean to Egypt.

Fighting continued until 31st May when the defenders surrendered their arms. House clearing in Cretan villages took a heavy toll of Fallschirmjäger lives.

On the German side - pyrrhic victory; 6,000 dead from a force of 22,000 men committed to the operation; 3,764 fatal casualties being airborne men. Of the 500 transport planes involved more than 250 were destroyed. The dead and wounded included many senior officers of XI Air Corps, among them the commander of 7th Air Division, General Süssmann, killed when the towing line of his glider snapped after barely leaving the ground. Scores of experienced officers at all levels of command were lost, as well as their NCO's; Braun, the Brigade-Major, Scherber, the commander of 3rd Battalion/Assault Regiment, and von Plessen, the glider specialist. The very 'spearhead' of the German 'lance', as Churchill put it, lay shattered.

Hitler for whom the élite parachutists were the embodiment of the Valkyrian mysticism, and who from the earliest days had taken a deep interest in airborne forces, declared to Student two months after the Battle of Crete 'the day of the parachutist is over. The Parachute arm is a surprise weapon and without the element of surprise there can be no future for airbone forces.'

In respect of German airborne offensive operations, Hitler's prediction at Wolfschanze turned out to be true. Although after Crete the Corps was rehabilitated and parachute forces fought with great determination in Russia, Tunisia, Italy and North West Europe, their employment was for the most part in the conventional ground rôle. Limited parachute operations were however carried out in the occupation of the island of Leros in 1943 and later in winter 1944 during the ill-fated Ardennes offensive.

The shortcomings of the Corps operation in Crete; need for heavy equipment, over-dependence on command of the air, heavy loss of transport planes and gliders and vulnerability on landing raised grave doubts in the mind of the German High Command as to the feasibility of operations such as 'Mercury' in the future. Ignoring the mistakes made by the defenders in their confusion, the parachutists had still come perilously close to failure. But for General Student's steady nerve and the timely redeployment of the 5th Mountain Division, the Air Division had faced the prospect of annihilation.

An important factor contributing to the German success was the complete lack of understanding by the British of the organisation, strength and equipment of German airborne troops. The British finally disposed of their uncertainties by the interrogation of captured parachutists and a close study of captured regimental orders and other military documents salvaged from the island. Hitler's negative pronouncement on the future of airborne troops can be understood in the context of Crete, but his attitude to the future of airborne operations was later proved to be wrong. The Germans did not believe that their enemies would engage in large scale airborne warfare; but the lessons of Crete not only apprised the Allies of the true potential of the airborne idea, but also how to use those lessons to good advantage.

How well the lessons had been grasped was proved by the Allied paratroop invasion of Sicily in July 1943. But as the point was progressively reinforced by the mass drops on D-Day in Normandy in June 1944, and later in Holland and on the crossing of the Rhine, so the

fortunes of the German airborne forces declined and the possibilities of large-scale airborne assault dwindled and finally died away. The Luftwaffe far from controlled the skies and transport planes were non-existent. When in Normandy an airborne counter-attack was proposed, the German High Command rejected the plan because the paratroopers were already in action on the ground.

Even before the capture of Crete was concluded the air transport groups were taken from XI Corps and redeployed in readiness for Operation 'Barbarossa'. The Stukas and long range fighters in Crete, the parachutists' mobile artillery, joined the four air fleets that were to be employed in the invasion of the USSR. On the ground three German army groups were marshalled in Poland for the advance across the Soviet border.

Crete strengthened with coastal artillery served as was Hitler's intention as a base for attacks against British shipping and also as a staging point for reinforcements and supplies destined for North Africa. The 7th Air Division returned to garrison towns at Braunschweig and Hildesheim, where they were welcomed as heroes. Student, Ramcke, Genz and Altmann were amongst those decorated for their achievements. But the buoyant mood of the parachutists was short-lived.

8 Military Operations — On Every Front

In Russia in the invasion so confidently set in motion on 22nd June 1941, German forces had by mid-November reached a line which extended from the gates of Leningrad in the north, southwards around the Valdai Hills before turning eastwards to Kalinin and thence southwards through Kharkov until it reached the Sea of Azov east of Mariupol.

These offensive operations, unparalleled in the history of warfare, were eventually brought to a halt as the fighting strengths of armoured and infantry regiments, engaged continuously for three months, were reduced by up to fifty per cent of their war establishment, and in certain instances to a quarter of this. Many units were no longer capable of attaining their military objectives.

Winter battles followed as Army Groups North and Centre fought to consolidate their positions round Leningrad and Moscow; OKW, the High Command of the Wehrmacht, committed 7th Air Division in piecemeal fashion as infantry reinforcement for the crucial sectors. Command of the division now lay with General Süssmann's successor, *Generalleutnant* Petersen.

At Leningrad, as part of the OKW plan to provide additional armoured support for a renewed attack on Moscow, *Generaloberst* Hoepner's Panzer Corps was withdrawn from the front on September 17th and switched south under command of Army Group Centre.

Into the vacuum created by the withdrawal of the Panzer Corps south and southwest of Schlüsselburg the Russians established bridgeheads across the Newa, first at Petruschino, threatening German Sixteenth Army's grip on the city, and then at Wyborgskaya, followed by serious incursions at Ssinzawino in the desolate snowbound forests of the Wolchow.

To counter these threats 2nd Battalion of the Assault Regiment, the first of the parachute units, was flown into the sector, followed later by FJR 1, FJR 3, ancillary artillery and engineer units and, later still, 7th Air Division headquarters.

After continuous and often bitter fighting the men of the Assault Regiment successfully eradicated the Newa bridgehead at Petruschino but at immense cost in lives, including that of their commander, *Major* Stenzler, the veteran of Hill 107 and Máleme. Every officer in the battalion was either killed or wounded in this action. The Parachute Engineer Battalion under *Major* Liebach with characteristic *élan* threw back numerous Russian attacks and successfully defended their posi-

USSR 1942, travelling leisurely by rail. A unit of the Assault Regiment whose emblem, a plunging star, is painted on the tailboard of their vehicle move to new positions on the East front.

tions at Ssinzawino and the 'Wasp's Nest' on the Newa. The two parachute regiments, FJR 1 and FJR 3, and the parachute anti-tank unit, were committed independently at numerous times in fierce and costly engagements. By the end of November much of the division, with the exception of FJR 2 engaged in the south and the Parachute MG Battalion on the central sector, were in action on the Northern front.

The six weeks' delay in the advance on Moscow, following the capture of Smolensk in August while the Germans operated on the flanks, was to prove fatal for the successful outcome of German military operations on the central sector, even with the help of Hoepner's Panzer Corps. Not only had the Russian winter caught up with the Germans but Stalin was given precious time in which to rush reserves to the

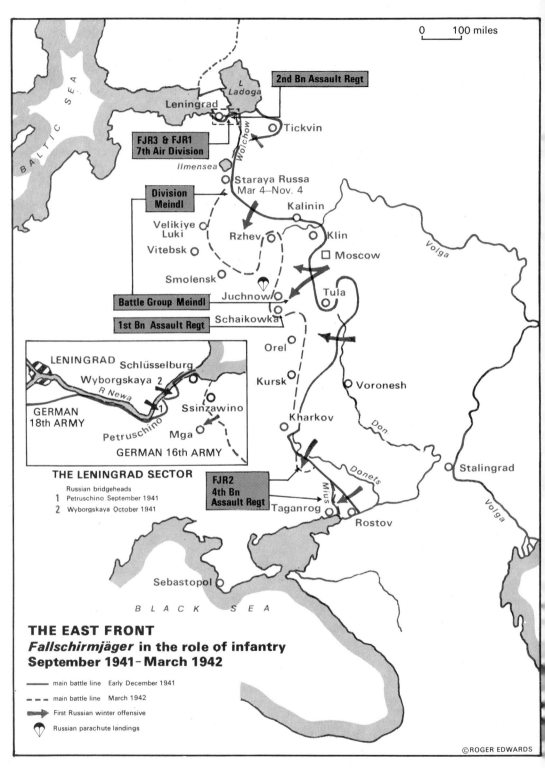

0   100 miles

2nd Bn Assault Regt

L Ladoga

Leningrad

Tickvin

**FJR3 & FJR1
7th Air Division**

Wolchow

Ilmensea

Staraya Russa
Mar 4–Nov. 4

Kalinin

**Division
Meindl**

Velikiye
Luki

Rzhev

Klin

Vitebsk

Moscow

Volga

Smolensk

Juchnow

Tula

Battle Group Meindl

Schaikowka

1st Bn Assault Regt

Orel

LENINGRAD   Schlüsselburg

Wyborgskaya 2

Kursk

Voronesh

R Newa

GERMAN
18th ARMY

Ssinzawino

Petruschino   Mga

Kharkov

Don

GERMAN 16th ARMY

THE LENINGRAD SECTOR

Russian bridgeheads
1 Petruschino September 1941
2 Wyborgskaya October 1941

**FJR2
4th Bn
Assault Regt**

Donets

Mius

Stalingrad

Taganrog

Rostov

Volga

Sebastopol

B L A C K   S E A

THE EAST FRONT
Fallschirmjäger in the role of infantry
September 1941– March 1942

— main battle line Early December 1941

--- main battle line March 1942

➤ First Russian winter offensive

Russian parachute landings

©ROGER EDWARDS

capital.

In December the first Soviet counter-offensive produced a deep salient across the Dvina in the direction of Vitebsk, disputing German possession there of the vital supply airfield at Schaikowka. The hazardous task of defending this installation was entrusted to 1st Battalion Assault Regiment commanded, as earlier in Crete, by *Major* Koch. Although frequently cut off from other ground support the battalion held the airfield throughout the winter, enduring not only the fierce attention of Siberian units but also winter temperatures that reached minus thirty degrees centigrade.

Elsewhere on the central sector in a salient that German Ninth Army had retained at Rzhev the Parachute Machine-Gun Battalion also endured the intense cold whilst withstanding Soviet attacks aimed at dislodging them from their exposed positions. At Juchnow the headquarters company of the Assault Regiment, reinforced by SS Regiment 4 and air force flak and ground personnel, although outflanked, fought under their regimental commander, *Generalmajor* Meindl, as Battle Group Meindl until the tide of Russian attacks finally turned in February 1942.

General Meindl later gathered several air force field regiments into Division Meindl and campaigned with immense determination in the area south of Staraya Russa where a Russian breakthrough threatened the German positions. The General's experience with air force regiments on the East front led him, as Corps Commander XIII Air Corps established at Grossborn, to the task of raising twenty-two new Luftwaffe field divisions for service in the East and in South East Europe. The corps staff were later to serve as the nucleus of 2nd Parachute Corps headquarters when by a change of name in winter 1943 the corps became responsible for raising new parachute divisions.

The Assault Regiment, General Meindl's former command, with its battalions distributed in crucial sectors along the entire length of the front – all, that is, except the 3rd Battalion which with *Major* Scherber was lost in Crete – could no longer fight as a complete formation and would never again be used *en masse* as it was during Operation 'Mercury'.

At the southern end of the front along the Mius River where the waterway helped to protect the German positions, FJR 2 with ancillary parachute units and 4th Battalion/Assault Regiment held the crossings against strong Soviet forces. Here, too, more of the highly trained parachutists fought doggedly as infantry, their grievous casualties bearing witness to the resolute spirit in which they undertook their defensive engagements. FJR 2, after a prolonged defence of their Mius position, were later transferred to the Wolchow and there in the marsh forests contributed significantly to the efforts of Sixteenth Army to withstand the Soviet spring offensive aimed at breaking the siege of Leningrad.

In their first winter of operations on the Eastern front 3,000 parachutists were either killed or wounded, many of them irreplaceable, battle-experienced veterans who had survived the attack on Holland and Crete; but with the spring thaw the parachute battalions were finally withdrawn for re-training and re-equipping in Northern France

USSR 1941, in the
suburbs of Leningrad.
Artillery and air
bombardment
reduced much of the
city to ruins. The
rubble from half
demolished buildings
afforded unexpected
opportunities for the
defence to impede the
advancing Germans, a
lesson that the
parachutists learned
well – as their
tenacious defence of
Cassino later so
convincingly affirmed.

USSR 1941/2.
Improvised sledges
aid the movement of
supplies and equip-
ment to units.
Personal camouflage
for winter operations
now consists of a
hooded jacket and
separate trousers.
Both are worn over
the standard field
uniform.

USSR 1941,
destruction at
Schaikowka. A
shattered Fieseler
Storch, Fi 156,
testifies to the
accuracy of Russian
gun-fire. A machine
such as this would
have been used for
artillery observation
or as personal
transport for senior
army and air-force
personnel.

and Central Germany.

In the late summer of 1942 it appeared likely that the division would be employed in an airborne rôle on the western flank of the Caucasus mountains. The task envisaged was to secure the approaches to Tuapse on the Black Sea ahead of Army Group A. The collapse of Field-Marshal List's armies however brought about the cancellation of the project. By the end of October the 7th Air Division was back in the line north of Smolensk and taking part in the battles raging at Velikiye-Luki and Orel.

While the paratroopers were campaigning as infantry in Russia, the staff of XI Air Corps was still examining the lessons of Crete. An answer was sought to the need for air-transported artillery: improvements were effected in the technique of delivering weapons to troops on the ground; also in the range and reliability of signals equipment. Plans were considered for strengthening and increasing the lifting capacity of the air transport groups by introducing new planes and gliders, especially the Gotha 242 and Me 323. In spite of Hitler's predictions after Crete, lengthy studies were undertaken of new opportunities for the employment of airborne forces, including the projected attacks on Malta, Gibraltar, the Cape Verde islands and Toulon harbour.

The Gibraltar project (Operation 'Felix') never amounted to more than a rather superficial plan for the occupation of the Rock by both parachute and air-landed troops. The plan was first conceived in the autumn of 1940, but was put aside and eventually considered again after the Allied landing in North Africa in 1942. The limited range of German transport and fighter planes called for airfields in Spain; but the Spanish government imposed unacceptable conditions on the Germans for the use of their airfields.

As regards the Toulon plan formulated in 1941 for occupying the

harbour, strong parachute detachments operating in conjunction with gliderborne troops were to be landed on the quayside and even if possible on the decks of the larger French ships lying at anchor. Coastal batteries commanding the harbour entrance would also have to be seized. The German intention of taking the French fleet by surprise was never carried out. As it happened most of the French ships in Toulon harbour were scuttled by their crews when the Germans occupied the whole of France after the Allied invasion of North Africa in November 1942.

The highest operational priority was given to Operation 'Hercules', the plan to capture Malta. The island fortress of Malta, from which British naval and air forces struck at Axis supply convoys to North Africa, was also a vital staging post for British supplies sent through the Mediterranean to Egypt.

In spring 1942 Hitler and Mussolini met at Obersalzburg to discuss the invasion of Malta. They agreed that, during the summer, the Italians would be by far the strongest partner in an invading army of six divisions. The landing was to be made in the wake of a combined Italo-German airborne assault with 30,000 men. *Generalmajor* Ramcke was despatched as chief instructor to the Italian *Folgore* Division and a month later General Student visited Rome to co-ordinate operational planning. The invading forces were to be under the command of the Prince of Piedmont. Aerial reconnaissance revealed the strength of Malta's anti-aircraft defences and fortifications and much additional information about the island. Intelligence staffs even knew the calibre of the coastal guns and measured the effect they would have if turned inwards on the invaders.

Gotha 242 gliders and the Me 321 which lifted 120 men or a field howitzer and its half track towing vehicle were assembled in readiness. Ten air-transport groups under *Generalmajor* Conrad with about 500 Ju 52's were assembled in Sicily. A total force of 100,000 men patiently awaited the signal to embark for Malta, which was defended by a British Imperial garrison of 30,000 men. The German plan was much the same as Operation 'Mercury'. The Maltese airfields and littoral were to be captured by the sky battalions; the initial phase being followed by a powerful seaborne invasion.

Meanwhile, a series of disasters had befallen General Auchinleck's British forces in the Western Desert. After attacking the Gazala-Bir Hacheim position in strength, General Rommel had driven all before him. On 21st June 1942 the mainly South African garrison at Tobruk was forced to surrender, and Auchinleck fell back to a defensive position extending from El Alamein to the Qattara Depression. Although Rommel's Panzer Army was now within striking distance of Cairo, his interior lines of communication were greatly extended. Fuel supplies so vital to his Panzer columns depended on long and hazardous sea voyages between Naples and Tripoli. Luftwaffe resources were greatly over-extended in Russia; and now with the build-up for Operation 'Hercules', fuel shortages greatly restricted German air support and supply operations in the Western Desert. Both sides were exhausted: the Germans mainly because of logistic difficulties; and the

A winter patrol wearing white smocks. Woollen balaclava helmets and woollen gloves help to ward off frostbite from which many units suffered more casualties than enemy gun-fire.

British by defeat in the field.

The recently promoted Field-Marshal Rommel still gambled on an early victory in Egypt, and on Hitler's insistence the air support allocated to Operation 'Hercules' was transferred to the Afrika Korps. Hitler, who anyway doubted the ability of the Italian navy to confront the British Mediterranean fleet, was not destined to raise the German flag over the Malta garrison. Rommel continued the attack, but an armoured thrust was parried by the Eighth Army at Alam el Halfa in late August. Sheltering in its *point d'appui* amongst military workshops in the sanctuary of the Nile Delta, the Eighth Army prepared for its greatest offensive, which was launched on the night of 23-24 October at El Alamein.

With the cancellation of Operation 'Hercules', a German parachute brigade was released along with the *Folgore* Division and despatched to Egypt. Ramcke's mixed German force of four parachute battalions with artillery, anti-tank and engineer support took station south of El Alamein near the Qattara depression. After Montgomery's massive artillery bombardment opened up on 23rd October, bitter fighting continued for several days, during which time both sides lost heavily and fortunes fluctuated. By 5th November when the attack was renewed in favour of the British, the parachutists found themselves cut off without any form of transport.

The paratroop brigade actually received orders to withdraw on 2nd November but although they had not been directly engaged, the dangers of their situation were all too apparent and the race to safety began. Wireless communications had now broken down completely and Ramcke had no way of knowing exactly how far the British advance had penetrated along the coastal road from El Alamein. Promptly seizing a British supply column and taking possession of its vehicles, the paratroopers on 7th November succeeded in reaching their own line, which had withdrawn as much as 185 miles by that time. For this exploit Ramcke was awarded the Oak Leaves to his Knight's Cross earned in Crete. Ramcke was later assigned in the rank of major-general to the task of raising a second parachute division at Nîmes in the South of France.

The Anglo-American invasion of French North Africa on 8th November 1942 in the rear of the Axis forces faced with the *debouchement* of the British Eighth Army from Egypt created new problems for the German Supreme Command. One solution appeared to be the employment of XI Air Corps, although limited in strength, as a highly mobile task force. Urgent representation from Berlin brought short-lived guarantees of support from French Vichy troops; all hostilities between the Allies and the French in Algeria and Morocco ceased on 11th November. By this time Allied forces were already advancing from the west into Tunisia.

In view of the early promises of the Vichy government, a swift parachute landing by FJR 5 was cancelled. Instead the regiment, now led by *Oberstleutnant* Koch, the veteran of Eban-Emael and formerly commander of the 1st Battalion/Assault Regiment, was ordered to Tunisia. The regiment immediately prepared to move with two of its battalions by rail and air from their training area in Normandy. In Athens a parachute company of the same regiment, commanded by *Hauptmann* Saur and earmarked for Ramcke's brigade, was instead given Tunisian reasssignment. Saur's orders were to secure the Tunisian airfields at La Marsa and El Aouina as points of entry for FJR 5 and other Luftwaffe units. Saur's detachment flying from Athens via Brindisi in Ju 52's landed at El Aouina on the morning of 9th November, and systematically occupied key points at both El Aouina and La Marsa. Saur was soon able to report to *Oberst* Harlinghausen, Air Officer Tunisia, that the mission had been successfully completed.

Assisted by newly-arrived Army troops and a company of Field-Marshal Kesselring's special 'guard' battalion from Rome, *Hauptmann* Saur's enlarged battle group raced for the port and harbour installations at Tunis. By 14th November the port facilities and city of Tunis were in German hands. The race for Tunis had been temporarily won. A rapid build-up of German military strength was quickly effected in Tunisia. FJR 5 arriving in the Naples area emplaned at nearby Caserta in the giant Me 323 transports.

The first company of the regiment arrived over Tunis as the airfield was under attack by British fighters. The newly formed XI Air Corps parachute engineer battalion led by *Major* Witzig, part of a 'scratch' regiment commanded by *Oberst* Barenthin, the Corps engineer specialist, was flown into Bizerta without loss. New Stuka and fighter groups also arrived. The 10th Panzer Division, an anti-aircraft division, and the Italian *Superba* Division were now earmarked for Tunisia. The massive German rearguard action being mounted in Tunisia between the Allied armies advancing from both west and east was commanded by General Nehring. Nehring was directly responsible to Field-Marshal Kesselring's command in Southern Europe.

Bizerta, Gabes, Sousa and other key locations were occupied and on 11th December the Allied advance in Tunisia was halted by Axis counter-attacks spearheaded by FJR 5 in the area of Medjez-el-Bab. In mid-February another powerful counter-attack was launched against the United States 2nd Corps, which was driven back about 50 miles between Faid Pass in the north and Gafsa in the south. The Germans advanced powerfully up to the Kasserine Pass but they were held and returned to their original positions in Tunisia by 3rd March.

Meanwhile, the British Eighth Army, after its victory at El Alamein, had made rapid progress. After capturing Tobruk on 13th November the 'Desert Rats' advanced through Benghazi, Tripoli, Mareth and took Gabes on 29th March. On 1st May the United States 2nd Corps on the left of the British First Army was poised for the drive on Bizerta. The Eighth Army with French troops on their left was ready to enter Tunis. On 13th May 1943 all the Axis forces laid down their arms. 240,000 prisoners were taken, the parachutists being included amongst the 125,000 Germans. *Generaloberst* von Arnim, of Army Group Africa, now the German commander in Tunisia, was amongst those captured. Erwin Rommel escaped to fight again. *Oberstleutnant* Koch had left North Africa before the German collapse.

For the German Supreme Command the North African campaign

had clearly illustrated the need for a highly trained mobile reserve, an assignment especially suited to XI Air Corps. At the time of need in Tunisia little more than a regiment could be raised for the battle. The Russian campaign entered a third year; the Germans recovered from disaster at Stalingrad and their second Russian winter.

In the foreseeable future the German Supreme Command must expect a *tour de force* hurled against the coastline of France. The need for a highly mobile, air-transported strategic reserve in the west was recognised and 7th Air Division was accordingly withdrawn from the Eastern front. Massive plans for the expansion of the Parachute Corps were however shelved.

As part of their contingency planning for the defence of Western Europe against Allied invasion, the Germans established special assembly points for parachute and gliderborne troops at airfields in the South of France. The rôle of airborne battalions was to land across lines of supply in the rear of enemy bridgeheads. Hopefully, the troops once on the ground would link up and create a barrier between the invaders and their sources of replenishment.

The area in the South of France selected for the specially equipped airfields was the Rhône delta. XI Air Corps Headquarters was transferred from Brittany. The movement of airborne troops to their billeting area was codenamed *Blaupunkt*. XI Air Corps was established in the Avignon area where the 7th Air Division, redesignated 1st Parachute Division in November 1942, was also stationed. The airfields at San Raphael and Hyères were made equipment centres but Istres was to be the focal point of the redeployment.

At Nîmes near Avignon the 2nd Parachute Division was being formed under *Generalmajor* Ramcke. *Generalmajor* Heidrich, former commander of FJR 3 assumed command of 1st Parachute Division. The Parachute Corps, with a combined strength of two divisions, plus Corps troops, totalled some 30,000 all ranks. Not since Crete had the airborne forces, all of them trained parachutists, been assembled under unified command. XI Air Corps Headquarters was also situated at Nîmes. 1st Parachute Division gave a parachute regiment (FJR 2) and a parachute artillery battalion to the 2nd Division. Two new parachute regiments (FJR 6 and FJR 7) were raised for the 2nd Division. Divisional parachute anti-tank, engineer and supply units were added and intensive training was carried out by both divisions, until mid-1943.

Extensive refitting demanded an adequate supply of new weapons. The cumbersome 3.7 cm. anti-tank gun was replaced by the more effective 7.5 cm. gun. Light guns in 7.5 cm. and 10 cm. calibres were issued to the parachute artillery battalions. The corps was adequately supported by the new tail-loading Gotha 240 glider easily capable of lifting the 7.5 cm. anti-tank gun and its crew.

Imbued with a new spirit XI Air Corps strove to achieve a new peak of efficiency. A new camouflage smock came into service. Supremely confident with their new weapons and equipment the two parachute divisions, comprising six regiments and ancillary units, were ready to meet any challenge. Confidence and morale were higher even than in the early days before Crete. Now hopefully the German eagle would

Fallschirmjäger
supported Afrika
Korps operations
south of El Alamein.
This photograph
illustrates typical
desert uniform. The
metal rod is used for
prodding below the
surface to locate anti-
personnel mines.

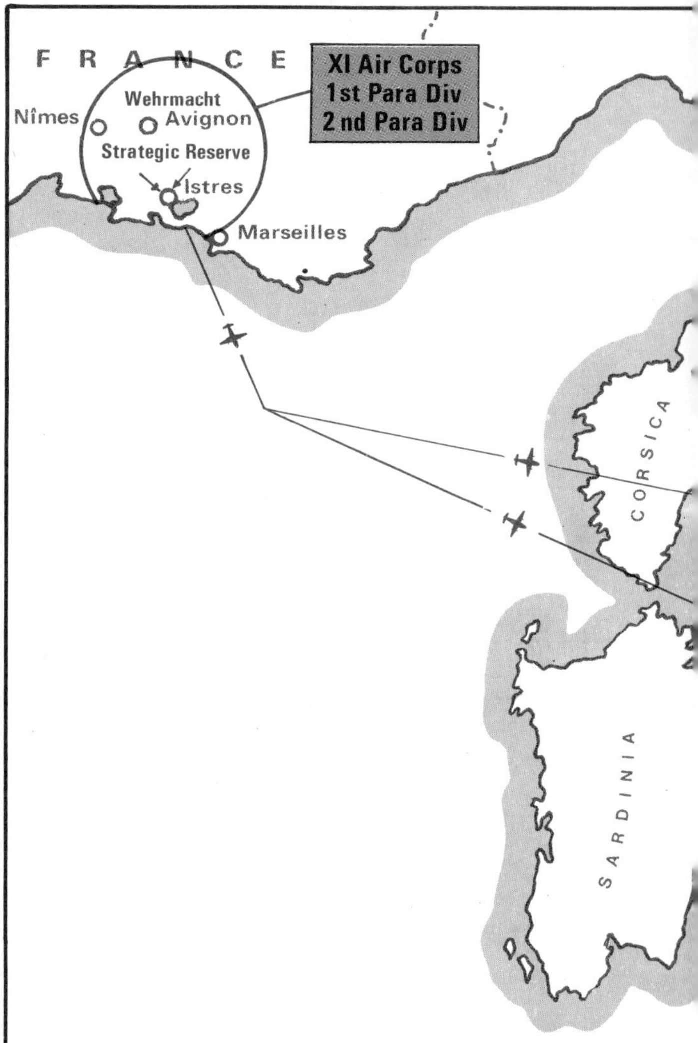

F R A N C E

| XI Air Corps |
| 1st Para Div |
| 2 nd Para Div |

Nîmes

Wehrmacht
Avignon
Strategic Reserve
Istres

Marseilles

CORSICA

SARDINIA

ITALY 1
Fallschirmjäger in the role of strategic reser
July 1943 - December 1943

Allied invasion armies

Allied airborne landings

German airborne response

German parachute/gliderborne landings

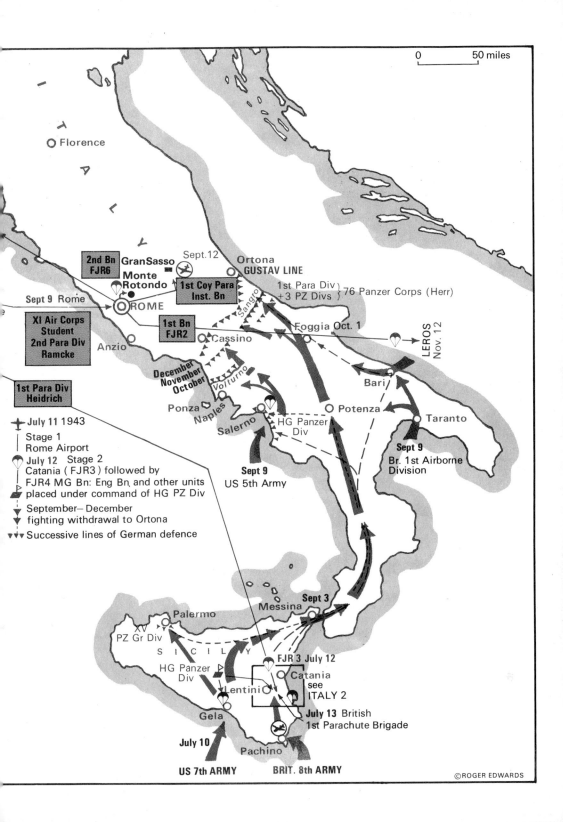

0   50 miles

O Florence

I T A L Y

2nd Bn FJR6   **GranSasso**   Sept.12   Ortona
GUSTAV LINE

Monte Rotondo   **1st Coy Para Inst. Bn**

1st Para Div) 76 Panzer Corps (Herr)
+3 PZ Divs)

Sept 9 Rome

ROME

XI Air Corps Student 2nd Para Div Ramcke

1st Bn FJR2   Cassino

Anzio

Foggia Oct. 1

LEROS Nov. 12

December November October

Volturno

Bari

1st Para Div Heidrich

Ponza

Naples

Salerno

Potenza

Taranto

HG Panzer Div

✠ July 11 1943

| Stage 1 Rome Airport

☮ July 12   Stage 2 Catania (FJR3) followed by FJR4 MG Bn: Eng Bn, and other units placed under command of HG PZ Div

▼ September—December fighting withdrawal to Ortona

▼▼▼ Successive lines of German defence

Sept 9 US 5th Army

Sept 9 Br. 1st Airborne Division

Sept 3

Messina

Palermo

XV PZ Gr Div

S I C I L Y

FJR 3 July 12

HG Panzer Div

Catania see ITALY 2

Lentini

July 13 British 1st Parachute Brigade

Gela

July 10

Pachino

US 7th ARMY   **BRIT. 8th ARMY**

©ROGER EDWARDS

rise phoenix-like as from the ashes of the desert and wastelands of Russia.

On 10th July 1943 the alarm was sounded. British, American and Canadian soldiers had landed in Sicily. 1st Parachute Division was alerted and within hours FJR 3 was on its way to Rome; landing swiftly at Catania on the east coast of Sicily. General Eisenhower's Allied forces consisted of Fifteenth Army Group under General Alexander, comprising the United States Seventh Army (Patton) and the British Eighth Army (Montgomery). The total force of 140,000 men included the Canadian 1st Division. The assault by sea was preceded by American and British airborne landings at Gela and Syracuse. The first Allied airborne operations on a big scale were only partially successful because of the stormy weather.

The German forces included the 15th Panzer Division with about sixty tanks and the Hermann Göring Division with about 100 tanks. The latter division had recently been rescued from Tunisia. The Italians had four divisions and 100 light tanks. In due course FJR 3 was joined by the 1st Parachute Machine-Gun Battalion, a detachment of artillery, 1st Parachute Engineers and part of 1st Parachute Anti-Tank Battalion. Finally the paratroopers were joined by their comrades from FJR 4. By 22nd July British Commonwealth forces had advanced northwards to the foothills of Mount Etna, while American troops had overrun the western part of the island. Only the northeast held out but by 17th August all Axis resistance had ended.

Events on the Italian mainland moved fast during the next few months. 1st Parachute Division was to see the fighting through until the bitter end of the following year. On 3rd September Montgomery's Eighth Army, with massive sea and air support, crossed the Straits of Messina and advanced rapidly northeastwards from Reggio against only light opposition. Mussolini had already been forced to resign and was held prisoner on the island of Ponza. Marshal Badoglio was ostensibly premier of Italy and King Victor Emmanuel III in command of the Italian Armed forces, but General Eisenhower announced on 8th September that a military armistice between the Allies and the Italian government had already been signed. On 9th September General Mark Clark's United States Fifth Army began landing south of Naples at Salerno. On 1st October the British 1st Airborne Divison, which had also landed on 9th September at Taranto, captured the important airfield of Foggia.

Several of the best Italian divisions had been stationed in Rome to protect the capital. Now in the chaos that reigned after the Italian surrender XI Air Corps, with the 2nd Parachute Division and later the 3rd Panzer Grenadier Division under Corps direction, on Hitler's urgent orders seized and held the Italian capital on 9th September. Rome was of course a vital communications centre for German divisions fighting in the south. General Student executed a series of brilliant actions in stabilising the situation in the Rome area; and contributed greatly to the confidence of the High Command in the ability of the German Army to hold its own in Italy. Amongst these actions must be noted the sharp attack by the 2nd Battalion of FJR 6 (*Major* Gericke) against the Italian

Army Headquarters at Monte Rotondo, which was overcome after spirited resistance.

On 12th September Mussolini, who was now to be found in a new place of confinement, was rescued by a brilliant gliderborne operation from his hiding place at the Hotel Albergo-Rifugio on the Gran Sasso plateau northeast of Rome. His whereabouts was discovered by SS *Obersturmbannführer* Otto Skorzeny, who discarded his first idea to use parachutists for the mission because of the thermal wind currents in the mountains. The mission was first approved and then controlled by General Student from the Practica di Mare airfield near Rome. Whilst on 8th September *Major* Mors' paratroop battalion captured the lower end of the funicular below the mountain lair, eight of Skorzeny's twelve DFS 230 gliders at the same time landed in the car park alongside the hotel. Skorzeny's mixed force of paratroopers and *Waffen* SS Special Forces – including the reluctant Italian General Soleti – successfully located the Duce, who was flown with Skorzeny in Student's personal Fieseler Storch to the Practica di Mare airfield. The former Italian leader was then flown in a Heinkel 111 to Vienna.

Five days later 2nd Battalion FJR 2 (Pietzonka) was ordered to occupy the island of Elba where the Italian garrison had acknowledged the terms of the armistice. The battalion jumped as planned in the neighbourhood of Portoferraio, the principal harbour, on the north coast of the island. After a sharp engagement assisted by a Stuka raid, the Italian force of 10,000 men laid down their arms.

Following the Italian capitulation the Dodecanese islands of Kos, Leros and Samos were taken by the Allies, but quickly recaptured by German army and air force battle groups. Kos fell to a seaborne landing by the army, and Leros after a four-day fight to a combined air and sea assault spearheaded by 1st Battalion FJR 2. The Allies were thus deprived of valuable 'jumping-off' grounds for an offensive in the Balkans.

At the end of 1943, 2nd Parachute Division was stationed in the Rome area and 1st Parachute Division was part in action and part resting on the Garigliano and Sangro rivers south and east of Rome. Delighted with Skorzeny's adventure Hitler now agreed to Goring's plan to expand XI Air Corps into a parachute army under the command of General Student. At an air staff conference in September 1943 at Karinhall, *Reichsfeldmarschall* Goring completed plans for raising 2nd Parachute Corps of two divisions plus Corps troops and ancillary services. Command of the new corps fell to *Generalmajor* Meindl, veteran commander of the Assault Regiment in Crete and presently commander of XIII Air Corps responsible for raising Luftwaffe field divisions. Many of Meindl's old colleagues, veterans of Fort Eban-Emael, were employed in the reconnaissance unit of XIII Air Corps, but purely on ground assignments. The assembly area agreed upon for 2nd Parachute Corps was the Melun district near Paris, where a new parachute training school existed at Dreux.

Young volunteers were accepted by their units after parachute training at Dreux and the other schools at Salzwedel, Wittstock and Kraljevo. NCO's and other ranks mainly from the demonstration

A member of the
Demonstration
Battalion poses for a
portrait after the
successful action to
free Mussolini. In the
background lies a
late production model
D.F.S. 230; carried
on the man is the
FG 42 and special
bandolier.

battalion of 1st Parachute Corps formed the kernel of FJR 8 and FJR 9, two new regiments that together with the reconstituted FJR 5 (lost in Tunisia) made up the main strength of 3rd Parachute Division (*Generalmajor* Schimpf). The 5th Parachute Division (*Generalmajor* Wilke) also consisted of three new regiments FJR 13, 14 and 15. Parachute artillery, anti-tank, engineer and medical units were raised in support of the new divisions. On completion of training 2nd Parachute Corps was posted to Brittany under German Seventh Army.

In Italy, meanwhile, the 4th Parachute Division had been formed from the former Italian *Nembo* and *Folgore* parachute divisions. Three parachute regiments, FJR 10, 11 and 12 with a cadre of experienced officers and men provided by the 2nd Parachute Division were raised by *Generalmajor* Heinz Trettner in the vicinity of Perugia. Thrown into the Battle of Anzio in late January 1944, the 4th Parachute Division was virtually raised in the heat of action.

1944 brought no respite for the *Fallschirmjäger*. The winter of 1943-1944 was a period of hard fighting which brought the Allies up to the German Gustav line. The American Fifth Army, including three British divisions, and the British Eighth Army, including Indian, Canadian and New Zealand divisions, were shortly joined by both the French and Polish Corps. In mid-October 1943 these massive heterogeneous forces were poised to prise the German army from their prepared positions on the Garigliano and Sangro rivers. Behind these natural barriers Field-Marshal Kesselring's forces were dug in south of Rome on the Gustav line, which extended for 100 miles westward across Italy, from the Sangro river south of Ortona on the Adriatic to the Tyrrhenian Sea near the mouth of the Garigliano river. The natural protection afforded by this mountainous region was supplemented by formidable defence works constructed with the help of the Todt organisation. The bastion of the Gustav line rose to a height of 1,500 feet alongside the main road to Rome through the Liri valley. This towering geographical feature, crowned by a Benedictine Monastery, is called Monte Cassino.

On 13th October the Fifth Army crossed the Volturno river and attacked in the Liri valley on 1st December. Meanwhile the Eighth Army on the right launched its offensive on the Sangro in mid-November. In order to assist the advance to Rome an amphibious Allied landing was made on 22nd January 1944 north of the Gustav line at Anzio. The immediate objective of the landing was to cut the communications of the German 14th Army. Savage fighting ensued both in the bridgehead at Anzio and along the Gustav line but it was nearly five months before Rome was captured. The Allies made no significant advance until the Polish Corps occupied the abbey at Monte Cassino on 18th May and the Anzio offensive was ordered five days later.

General Heidrich's 1st Parachute Division relieved General Baade's 90th Panzer Grenadier Division at Cassino on 29th February. During the next ten weeks the paratroopers were subjected to continual bombardments by heavy bombers as well as by artillery. Since January two principal attacks had been launched against this position by American,

New Zealand, Indian and British troops. The paratroopers dug in to await the next assault on the town and on the heights, a human locking pin in the Gustav defensive system.

At Anzio Kesselring concentrated ten German divisions against the four Allied divisions that had scrambled ashore. The 4th Parachute Division, so recently formed from the two Italian parachute divisions, participated in the vigorous efforts of the German Fourteenth Army to collapse the bridgehead. The United States VI Corps (Lucas) expanded the bridgehead to 18 miles in width and 9 miles in depth, but instead of driving through the Alban hills was content to consolidate the bridgehead that existed until late May.

From the very first days at Anzio the 4th Parachute Division was in the forefront of the fighting. The Hermann Göring Panzer Division was also severely tested at this time. A battle-group of three parachute companies first engaged the enemy at Aprilia Factory near Carroceta on the road leading north from Anzio. More units of the 4th Division arrived at the front, and by 16th February the paratroopers were partnered in the field by 64th Infantry Division to form 1st (Parachute) Corps. The Corps bit deeply into the left wing of the Allied flank driving Scottish Highland troops out of their positions at Carroceta. Further attacks were attended by less than spectacular success; the Allies held on firmly to their entrenchment south of Rome and the German Fourteenth Army was quite unable to throw them back into the sea. For the Allies the success of the bridgehead was measured by the number of German divisions that they succeeded in tying down in the Anzio area.

At Cassino on 15th March more than 1,000 tons of high explosive and fragmentation bombs cascaded on to the town from 500 heavy and medium bombers from the United States Strategic Air Force. Where the United States 2nd Corps (the 34th and 36th Divisions), the New Zealand 2nd Corps, Indian 4th, and British 78th Divisions had earlier failed, the Allies attempted to obliterate the defences and break through to Rome.

Heilmann's FJR 3 dug into and around the town endured the full weight of the bombing. 800 guns heralding the infantry attack added to the holocaust. The ground shuddered, seemingly, under the impact of a thousand express trains. Buildings collapsed and bodies were torn apart by shrapnel. The New Zealand 2nd and Indian 4th Divisions stormed into the town fighting at close quarters with the *Fallschirmjäger*; even attempting to establish posts in the same houses.

The New Zealanders occupied the railway station and Gurkha troops, who had recently been in action on the Sangro, attempted to storm the heights. The nimble soldiers from Nepal were at home in the mountains and they pushed on successfully to Hangman's Hill. Having established a strongpoint inside the German positions, the Gurkhas were obliged to withdraw from the exposed hill location under devastating enfilade fire. The New Zealanders held the railway station for a time, but the third great attack on Cassino had failed.

Losses on both sides were heavy. Of the 300 men in 2nd Battalion FJR 3, 200 were killed mainly as a result of the bombing. In the fighting on the Cassino sector during February and March, Indian and Gurkha casualties alone amounted to 3,000 men. General Alexander, the Allied Commander-in-Chief in Italy, paid tribute to the steadfast and resolute spirit of the defence in the following words: 'The power of resistance of the German *Fallschirmjäger* is extraordinarily remarkable for one must consider that they were exposed to the bombardment of our combined available air power and the shelling from about 800 guns for six hours – the heaviest bombardment that has ever been undertaken. I doubt whether there is another unit in the world that would endure that and continue fighting with the same doggedness as these people.'

The fourth and last assault on the Cassino position was carried out on 11th May by the Polish Corps, with the British 2nd Corps on its left ready to advance up Highway 6 in the Liri Valley and open the road to Rome. Farther to the left the Fifth Army (which included the French Corps) was to advance on Rome, using Highway 7 as its main axis. The offensive was supported by 1,000 guns with the Eighth Army and 600 with the Fifth Army and by more than 3,000 planes. The centres of pressure lay to the north and south of Cassino.

The 1st Parachute Division after a temporary rest period was back in the line. (The 2nd Parachute Division by this time was in the Ukraine supporting the withdrawal of Army Group A.) FJR 4 held the town and monastery; FJR 3 the neighbouring areas of Monte Caira and Collo San Angelo, where *Gebirgsjäger* of 100 Mountain Regiment were placed under airborne command. 100 Mountain Regiment was part of Ringel's Mountain Division, which had fought alongside the 7th Air Division in Crete. FJR 1 stood in reserve behind both regiments.

The heaviest engagement was at Collo San Angelo, where General Anders, the Polish Corps commander, threw in his 5th Polish Division in a bid to capture the heights. All attempts to take the high ground were frustrated by 2nd Battalion FJR 3; but the parachutists' position at the monastery was seriously threatened when a parachute rifle detachment on Hill 593 was overwhelmed by troops from the 3rd Polish (Carpathian) Division. Four counter-attacks by the reserve companies failed to restore the situation for the Germans, but a fifth rally led by *Oberfeldwebel* Schmidt of the 14th Company recovered the hill and the Germans held on firmly against further Polish attacks. The 1st Parachute Division was ordered to withdraw from Cassino on the night of 17th May.

Meanwhile the French Corps, a mixed force of Algerian and Moroccan Colonial troops, had suceeded in outflanking the Gustav line southwest of Cassino at Itri. The whole Allied battlefront westward from Cassino then surged forward and events moved rapidly. With XIV Panzer Corps retreating before the French North Africans on the southwestern sector, Field-Marshal Kesselring OB (*Oberbefehlshaber*) South and General von Vietinghoff, 10th Army commander, discussed hasty plans to establish the Hitler line further back. The 'line' had been crossed however before their plans were finalized.

Sensing victory the Allied commander ordered the breakout from the Anzio-Nettuno bridgehead. Aided by fresh troops notably the United States 36th Division the Anzio offensive on 23rd May was completely

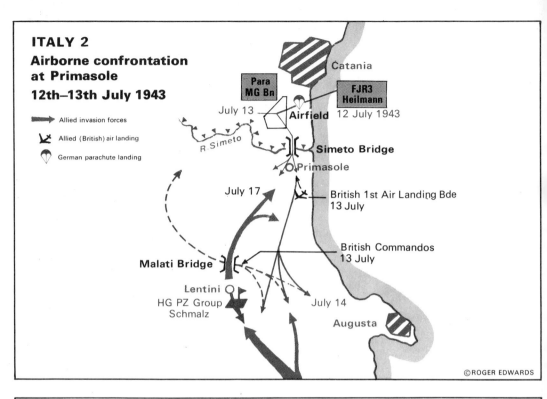

ITALY 2
Airborne confrontation at Primasole
12th–13th July 1943

➤ Allied invasion forces

⤬ Allied (British) air landing

⛴ German parachute landing

Catania

Para MG Bn

FJR3 Heilmann

July 13

Airfield   12 July 1943

R. Simeto

Simeto Bridge

Primasole

July 17

British 1st Air Landing Bde
13 July

British Commandos
13 July

Malati Bridge

Lentini

HG PZ Group Schmalz

July 14

Augusta

©ROGER EDWARDS

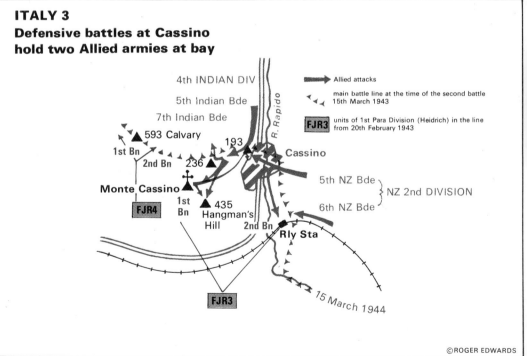

ITALY 3
Defensive battles at Cassino hold two Allied armies at bay

4th INDIAN DIV

5th Indian Bde

7th Indian Bde

➤ Allied attacks

◄◄ main battle line at the time of the second battle
15th March 1943

FJR3 units of 1st Para Division (Heidrich) in the line
from 20th February 1943

▲ 593 Calvary

R. Rapido

1st Bn

2nd Bn

236 ▲

193 ▲

Cassino

Monte Cassino ✝

FJR4

1st Bn

▲ 435
Hangman's Hill

2nd Bn

5th NZ Bde

6th NZ Bde

} NZ 2nd DIVISION

Rly Sta

FJR3

15 March 1944

©ROGER EDWARDS

122

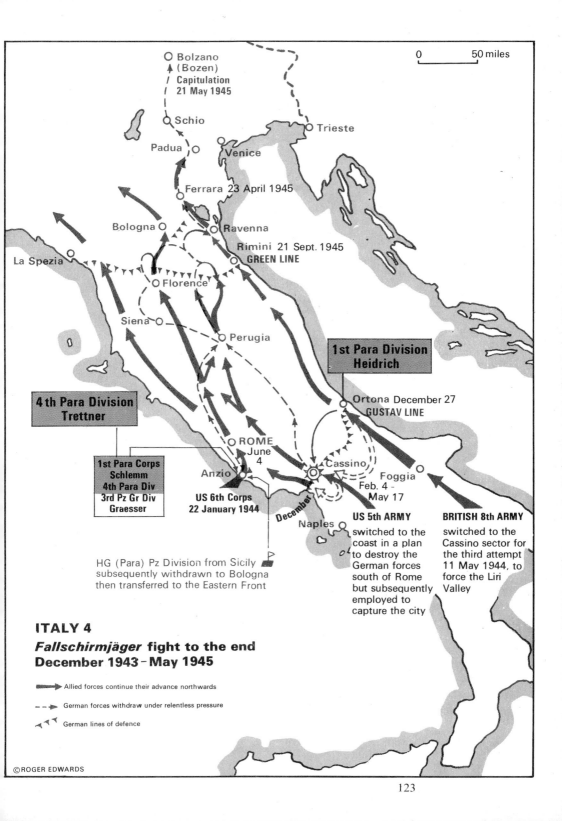

O Bolzano
(Bozen)
Capitulation
21 May 1945

O Schio

Padua O   O Venice   O Trieste

O Ferrara 23 April 1945

Bologna O   O Ravenna

Rimini 21 Sept. 1945
GREEN LINE

La Spezia O

O Florence

Siena O

O Perugia

**1st Para Division
Heidrich**

**4 th Para Division
Trettner**

Ortona December 27
GUSTAV LINE

O ROME
June
4

**1st Para Corps
Schlemm
4th Para Div
3rd Pz Gr Div
Graesser**

Anzio O

Cassino

Foggia
Feb. 4 -
May 17

**US 6th Corps
22 January 1944**

December

Naples O

US 5th ARMY
switched to the
coast in a plan
to destroy the
German forces
south of Rome
but subsequently
employed to
capture the city

BRITISH 8th ARMY
switched to the
Cassino sector for
the third attempt
11 May 1944, to
force the Liri
Valley

HG (Para) Pz Division from Sicily
subsequently withdrawn to Bologna
then transferred to the Eastern Front

0   50 miles

ITALY 4
Fallschirmjäger fight to the end
December 1943 – May 1945

Allied forces continue their advance northwards

German forces withdraw under relentless pressure

German lines of defence

©ROGER EDWARDS

successful. At Valletri where previously FJR 12 had denied the United States 34th Division entry into the Alban Hills, 6th Corps secured a wide breach between the two besieging German corps. 1st Parachute Corps was bypassed at Valletri, XIV Panzer Corps screening the retreat of the German Tenth Army. Disaster faced two German armies on the Italian front, but Kesselring's forces did not completely disintegrate when their principal positions at Anzio and Cassino collapsed.

On 4th June American troops of General Mark Clark's Fifth Army entered Rome almost eleven months after the Allied landing in Sicily. 1st and 4th Parachute Divisions were to remain in Italy with 1st Parachute Corps until the German capitulation in May 1945. At Florence, Rimini and Bologna and finally on the Po the parachutists strongly contested the Allied advance. The parachute divisions were proud of their conduct of military operations in the Italian campaign; but Anzio and Cassino unquestionably took pride of place in their list of battle honours.

On 6th June, two days after Rome was entered, the Allies launched Operation 'Overlord' against the German armies in Northern France. Following the airborne landings by the United States 82nd and 101st Divisions on the Cotentin Pensinsula and the British 6th Airborne Division's landing between the Ornes and Dives river, the United States 4th Division under 7th Corps touched down on the Omaha and Utah beaches southeast of Cherbourg.

British and Canadian troops of the British Second Army also made successful landings on 6th June further east on Gold, Juno and Sword beaches near Bayeux. By the end of D-Day the Allies had apparently established solid footholds on the Continent. Priority was given to the task of linking the two American bridgeheads and the link-up of Bradley's First Army and on their left Dempsey's Second Army facing Bayeux and Caen.

On the German side Field-Marshal von Runstedt controlled two Army Groups in France. Field-Marshal Rommel's Army Group B held Brittany, Normandy and the Pas-de-Calais. Hausser's Seventh Army now faced the lodgement area occupied by General Eisenhower's invading armies. By 1st July almost 1,000,000 Allied troops had been landed in France. The line had penetrated 20 miles in depth and extended a distance of some 75 miles from the Cherbourg Peninsula to the coast east of Sword beach and the first phase of the invasion had come to an end.

Generalleutnant Eugen Meindl's 2nd Parachute Corps with 3rd and 5th Parachute Divisions was moved from Brittany and assembled at St Lô facing Bradley's American sector. Continually harassed by fighter bombers the parachutists first skirmished with the United States 2nd Infantry Division as the former took station at St Lô, an important road and rail junction town 20 miles inland from Omaha beach. But Rommel's golden opportunity to smash the invasion by decisive counter-attack before the Allies were firmly established had passed.

The British were seemingly stalled before Caen, but Bradley's First Army stepped up the pressure in the area south of Cherbourg. Attempting to break out of their bridgehead on 11th July four American

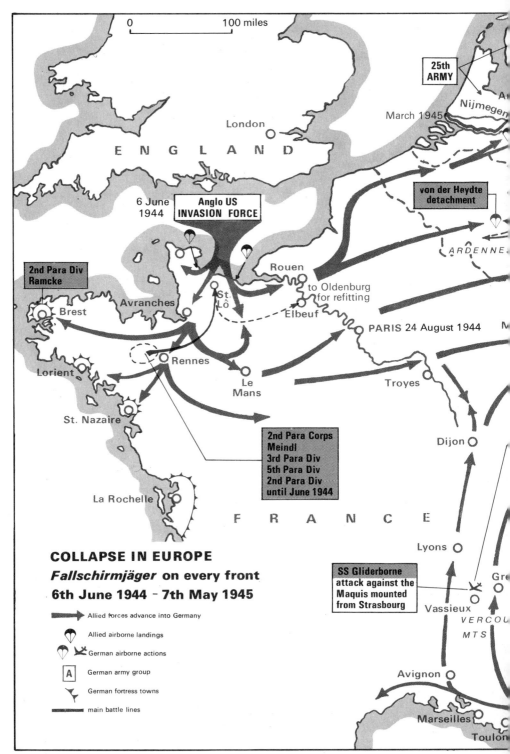

0   100 miles

25th
ARMY

Nijmegen

March 1945

London

E N G L A N D

6 June
1944

Anglo US
INVASION FORCE

von der Heydte
detachment

Rouen

ARDENNE

2nd Para Div
Ramcke

to Oldenburg
for refitting

St.
Lô

Avranches

Brest

Elbeuf

PARIS 24 August 1944

Rennes

Lorient

Le
Mans

Troyes

St. Nazaire

2nd Para Corps
Meindl
3rd Para Div
5th Para Div
2nd Para Div
until June 1944

Dijon

La Rochelle

F R A N C E

Lyons

COLLAPSE IN EUROPE
Fallschirmjäger on every front
6th June 1944 – 7th May 1945

SS Gliderborne
attack against the
Maquis mounted
from Strasbourg

Gre

Vassieux

VERCO

MTS

Avignon

Marseilles

Toulon

Allied forces advance into Germany

Allied airborne landings

German airborne actions

A   German army group

German fortress towns

main battle lines

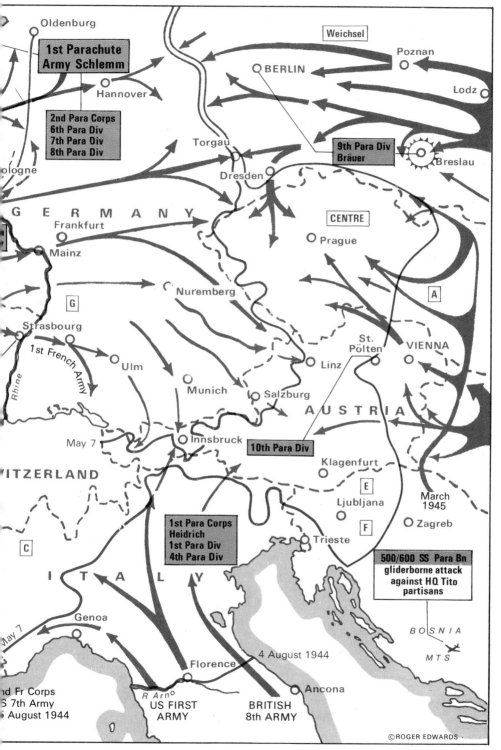

Oldenburg

1st Parachute Army Schlemm

Hannover

**2nd Para Corps
6th Para Div
7th Para Div
8th Para Div**

Weichsel

Poznan

○ BERLIN

Lodz

Torgau

**9th Para Div
Bräuer**

Breslau

Dresden

ologne

G E R M A N Y

Frankfurt

CENTRE

○ Prague

Mainz

A

Nuremberg

G

Strasbourg

St. Pölten

VIENNA

1st French Army

Ulm

Linz

Rhine

Munich

Salzburg

A U S T R I A

May 7

Innsbruck

10th Para Div

Klagenfurt

WITZERLAND

E

March 1945

Ljubljana

**1st Para Corps
Heidrich
1st Para Div
4th Para Div**

Zagreb

F

C

Trieste

**500/600 SS Para Bn
gliderborne attack
against HQ Tito
partisans**

I T A L Y

Genoa

B O S N I A

May 7

M T S

Florence

4 August 1944

nd Fr Corps
S 7th Army
August 1944

R Arno

US FIRST ARMY

Ancona

BRITISH 8th ARMY

©ROGER EDWARDS

corps were strongly resisted by Hausser's Seventh Army. FJR 9 and FJR 13 were particularly hard hit, the latter losing its commander, *Major* von Schulenburg. FJR 6 seconded from 2nd Parachute Division gave distinguished service in support of the 17th SS Panzer Grenadier Division, Gotz von Berlichingen. The parachutists continued to strengthen their positions at St Lô, but the town fell to the American 19th Corps on 18th July.

On 25th July Operation 'Cobra' achieved a breakthrough west of St Lô, where the advance was preceded by an aerial bombardment of great intensity. The 2nd Parachute Corps west of St Lô at first appeared to be holding, but the Americans threw in two extra divisions to assist the First Army's breakthrough, and a tremendous breach was opened. The parachutists suffered heavy casualties, including *Major* Stephani who commanded FJR 9.

The Americans took Avranches and gained the base of the Cotentin Peninsula. The breakthrough not only opened the gateway to Brittany, but also enabled the First Army to swing east towards the Seine river and Paris. The German left flank had been crushed. The American forces were now greatly strengthened when the First Army (now Hodges) was joined by Patton's Third Army which became operational on 1st August. As elements of the Third Army turned west from Avranches and entered Brittany the plight of the German army in Normandy became acute.

If Montgomery's forces drove southward from the Caen area to Falaise, the Allies would form a pocket and threaten the German Seventh and Fifth Panzer Armies with encirclement. Accordingly Crerar's Canadian First Army struck southward on 8th August but at first gained little ground. American 15th Corps advancing from the west took Alençon and was soon within sight of Argentan. The only escape route for the German forces lay through the 15-mile Argentan-Falaise gap.

2nd Parachute Corps along with the Seventh Army was virtually trapped. In the pocket with XVII Panzer Corps and the remains of thirteen other divisions, the parachutists joined forces with the army in a determined effort to escape. General Meindl and his staff, divisional and corps troops were assembled together with individual battle groups to make the break. The Allies made contact at Chambois and Trun on 20th August and the gap was closed. The parachutists, including General Meindl and General Schimpf (of 3rd Parachute Division), had for the most part got away. General Hausser himself escaped with the help of the parachutists. But when the pocket closed 10,000 German troops had been killed, 50,000 were now captured and the remnants of the Seventh and Fifth Panzer Armies sent staggering across the Seine in retreat.

In Brittany 2nd Parachute Division recalled from the Ukraine stubbornly defended the Atlantic port of Brest against Middleton's American 8th Corps. Siege operations were initiated on 25th August. Inside the port FJR 2 and FJR 7 were in the midst of the battle that raged for three weeks. *Generalmajor* Ramcke, the divisional commander, assumed command of all forces in the area.

The destruction of the port facilities at Brest denied to the Americans the use of a port that had been earmarked as an immediate point of entry for troops and supplies sent directly across the Atlantic from the United States. The Brest fortress was cleared of its defenders on 20th September. General Ramcke, who was awarded the Swords and Diamonds to his Oak Leaves and Knights Cross, went into American captivity.

On 15th August the Allies staged another amphibious invasion, this time on the south coast of France between Cannes and Toulon. The subsequent drive north exceeded all expectations, but having reached the foothills of the Vosges the Germans turned to fight back. The main Allied armies in the north having captured Paris jumped the Seine on 25th August and continued to pursue the Germans across northern France and Belgium towards the German border. Bradley sent Hodges' First Army northwards alongside the flank of Montgomery's 21st Army Group. While Patton's Third Army advanced alone south of the Ardennes, the Canadians invested the Channel ports and the British occupied Brussels on 3rd September.

On the Eastern front, where so many parachutists had given their lives, Leningrad had been relieved and the Crimea freed by 22nd June 1944, and Soviet troops had crossed the Rumanian border. German losses were needlessly heavy. In the second half of 1944 the Russians struck several great blows concurrently with the Allied offensives in France and Italy. An attack through Minsk drove 250 miles in three weeks and destroyed two German armies. A blow in the north cleared Estonia, Lithuania and most of Latvia; another in the south carried to the gates of Budapest, forcing Rumania and Bulgaria out of the war. On 3rd October British commando and airborne troops landed in southern Greece. As the year closed the Italian battlefront was generally inactive, but on 28th December the Germans launched a powerful counter-attack in the Serchio valley.

Partisan groups operating both as large armies and small groups of saboteurs were a serious threat to the retreating German armies especially in Yugoslavia and France. Two German airborne operations were planned to remove these threats, and it was only by chance that the first failed to realise its objectives. Operation 'Rösselsprung' was launched in spring 1944 with the intention of capturing Marshal Tito in his mountain hideout in the Drvar district of Bosnia. The newly raised 500 SS *Fallschirmjäger* Battalion was entrusted with the task. This unit, which was largely made up from military offenders from an SS rehabilitation battalion, was commanded by SS *Haupsturmführer* Rybka.

Tito's battle headquarters lay in virtually inaccessible mountain terrain. On 25th May gliderborne and parachute troops of 500 Battalion were landed in the Drvar district supported by mountain troops and other Wehrmacht and SS units. Despite the successful location of Tito's headquarters, which had been established in a cave, the glider troops delegated for Tito's capture met their end when their glider crashed on landing. The great Yugoslav partisan leader fled with his staff into the forests and ultimately reached safety on the Italian mainland.

500 SS Battalion suffered very heavy losses when their relief column, expected within 24 hours, was delayed by partisan action. The SS units were encircled and also lost many of their number. The survivors of 500 Battalion were reformed into 600 SS *Fallschirmjäger* Battalion; and in recognition of the merits of their action their SS insignia was restored; their rehabilitation was complete.

In the second and more successful airborne operation, tactics of a similar kind were employed against French resistance groups south of Grenoble in the Vercors district of the French Alps. The 157th Infantry Division, supported by an air-landing unit, was given the task of flushing the Maquis from their Alpine redoubt. In July twenty gliders towed by Ju 52's set down half of the force at Vassieux, the remainder at nearby hamlets suspected of harbouring resistance fighters. Dropping zones from which arms and equipment had been distributed to the Maquis were captured. Partisan operations were thus seriously dislocated.

These examples of qualified German successes in hindering the activities of resistance groups illustrate the value of surprise so essential to airborne operations. Both engagements also demonstrate the effectiveness of air-landing action against insurgents; an echo of the British operation in 1932 when troops were lifted in air transports into action against the troublesome tribesmen in Iraq.

First Parachute Army was formed in March 1944 by upgrading XI Air Corps, at first under the command of General Student but later under General Schlemm. The new parachute army became operational in Holland during September. Four new parachute divisions were raised from Luftwaffe and Army personnel: they were 6th, 7th and 8th Parachute Divisions and a reformed 2nd Parachute Division. The 3rd and 5th Parachute Divisions were also reformed from survivors of the Normandy catastrophe. Two parachute assault gun battalions were raised and the Hermann Göring Panzer Division was bracketed with a new Hermann Göring Panzer Grenadier Division. These divisions were brought into the framework of the parachute army as the Hermann Göring Panzer Corps. Two more parachute divisions, 9th and 10th, were also raised at the end of the war but, like the HG Panzer Corps, did not serve directly with the parachute army.

As patrols of the U.S. First Army crossed the German frontier on 11th September and the troops from the invasion of southern France linked with those from Overlord, an early end to the war not only seemed probable but possible. General Eisenhower rejected the views of Montgomery and Patton on methods of approach into Germany, but sanctioned a plan to use three Allied airborne divisions to help the British Second Army across three major river obstacles in Holland: the Maas, Waal and Lower Rhine. In the meantime the Sixth Army Group, using separate supply routes, was to drive through the Vosges to the Upper Rhine.

The big airborne attack, labelled Operation Market began on 17th September. Brereton's First Allied Airborne Army, three divisions – the British 1st and the United States 82nd and 101st – landed near Arnhem Nijmegen and Eindhoven in the largest parachute operation of the war

Hitler had already brought General Student's First Parachute Army into the area south of Arnhem, where the *Fallschirmjäger* stood astride Hell's Highway (Eindhoven – Grave – Nijmegen). First Parachute Army was augmented by fleeing troops and several divisions of the Fifteenth Army. The Allied airborne troops were to seize a narrow corridor 65 miles deep to enable Dempsey's Second Army, in a companion ground attack called Operation Garden, to pass through and reach the Zuider Zee.

At Arnhem in the north the British airborne troops were pinned down by the 9th and 10th SS Panzer Divisions to a narrow bridgehead north of the Lower Rhine. The arrival of the Independent Polish Parachute Brigade south of the river was delayed by bad weather. For the Germans the situation was the reverse of Crete. In Operation 'Mercury' the 7th Air Division had been lucky to escape an immediate counter-attack. Field-Marshal Model, whose headquarters was actually situated near Arnhem, did not make the same mistake and threw in elements of the two nearby Panzer divisions. On 25-26 September the 2,000 survivors from an original force of about 11,000 men withdrew to the south bank of the river. The lessons of Crete had been learnt well by the Germans.

Although the airborne drops at Nijmegen and Eindhoven had been successful, the pursuit was temporarily halted and the Allied armies had run into trouble. On Sunday 17th September Student's headquarters was situated near the Wilhelmina Canal at Vught about ten miles west of Hell's Highway; and he was summoned to witness descents by American paratroopers from both Gavin's 82nd and Taylor's 101st Airborne Divisions. (As it happened Student did not remain in the house for long. An officer of the Belgian squadron of the SAS Brigade identified the house in a signal to SAS HQ at Moor Park in Hertfordshire and the Royal Air Force arrived to destroy the house within three hours. The officer who was named Kirschen had parachuted with his patrol into the area five days previously.)

Generaloberst Student now went on to Army Group H in Eastern Holland. The First Parachute Army (Schlemm) – the 2nd, 6th, 7th and 8th Divisions – along with the newly-formed Twenty-fifth Army hotly contested the Allied advance in the battles that followed. The full weight of the First Canadian Army (Crerar) and British 30th Corps (Horrocks) was taken by the 7th (Erdmann) and 8th (Wadehn) Parachute Divisions supported by Panzer and Panzer Grenadier Regiments. The Germans fought tenaciously until 8th November, inflicting 13,000 casualties on the Canadian First Army.

It took all the rest of November and part of December 1944 for the American First and Ninth Armies to build up their forces along the Roer River; but on 16th December Hitler struck back with his long-planned counter-offensive. Hitler's ambitious plan was to strike with three armies through the Ardennes forest, cross the Meuse River and recapture Antwerp, thereby sealing off four Allied armies in the north. Before dawn on 16th December, the Sixth SS and Fifth SS Panzer Armies as well as the Seventh Army totalling twenty-five divisions struck along 70 miles of the Ardennes front thinly manned by six American divisions.

Holland 1945; a reflection on the state of German airborne forces in the closing stages of the war. Radio equipment, weapons and personal effects transported by wheelbarrow.

Schimpf's 3rd Parachute Division went into the assault with Sepp Dietrich's Sixth SS Panzer Army towards Malmédy on the northern part of the sector. A battle group under *Oberst* von der Heydte mounted the last German parachute drop of the war in advance of the Sixth SS Panzer Army. Part of the airborne force, due to navigational errors and lack of experience in dropping parachutists, came down miles from the target. The advancing army never reached the remnants of the battle group and after six days the paratroopers surrendered to the Americans.

In the centre of the Ardennes sector Manteuffel's Fifth SS Panzer Army struck hard at Middleton's 8th Corps and made good progress towards Bastogne. At the southern end Brandenberger's Seventh Army was strengthened by Heilmann's 5th Parachute Division. Everywhere the Germans broke through but at terrible cost. The most notable success occurred south of St Vith, where on the second day the Panzer Corps headed towards the Meuse river by way of the Belgian town of Bastogne. The breakthrough beyond Malmédy was spearheaded by Peiper's First SS Panzer Division supported by Skorzeny's *Panzerbrigade 150*. Skorzeny's group was made up from English-speaking German volunteers dressed in American uniforms: they carried American equipment and travelled in American vehicles and in disguised Sherman tanks with markings of the United States 5th Armoured Division. Hastened to the defence of Bastogne on 18th December, the American 82nd Airborne Division held off all attacks until relieved by the American 4th Armoured Division on 3rd January.

Eisenhower put all forces north of the Ardennes bulge under Field-Marshal Montgomery, while General Bradley retained command of the forces to the south. The German Panzer divisions were still a long way from the Meuse when on 23rd December the Allied fighter bombers roared into the attack, and by the 25th Hodges' First Army had established an unyielding line north of the Amblève river. Efforts to link

132

the American First with the Third Army in the south in a pincer grip around the German armoured columns succeeded when patrols from the two armies met on 16th January at Houffalize. The American pincers failed however to trap sizeable numbers of German troops, who fell back to the German frontier.

The Battle of the Bulge was the greatest pitched battle on the Western front in the Second World War. A total of twenty-nine German and thirty-three Allied divisions (mainly American) participated. The Panzers had created a short-lived bulge in the American line, 70 miles wide and 50 miles deep at its western-most point. The loss of priceless reserves left the German Army wide open once the Allies resumed their offensive in earnest.

As the First and Third Armies eliminated the last of the bulge at the end of December, preparations for the drive to the Rhine began in earnest. On 8th February the Canadian First Army attacked from positions near Nijmegen southeastwards and up the west bank of the Rhine. Simpson's Ninth Army on 12th February jumped the Roer and gained the Rhine near Düsseldorf before turning northwards to link with the Canadians. Dempsey's British Second Army pushed eastwards between the two armies. Parachute divisions stood resolutely in defence along the path of the Second Army, earning the greatest respect from their adversaries, including Field-Marshal Montgomery. Stiff fighting occurred at Venlo, in the Reichswald, and further south on German territory at Geldern, Rees and Emmerich. First Parachute Army next engaged British troops when they first crossed the Rhine at Wesel.

Mixed battle groups of *Generaloberst* Student's Army Group H took a heavy toll of British and Canadian soldiers. At Kappeln the destruction of Allied armour by a modest battle group of parachutists from 12th Parachute Assault Gun Brigade is one of the most remarkable on record. No fewer than 100 armoured vehicles were destroyed, severely damaged or otherwise put out of action.

After the Ardennes failure the 3rd and 5th Parachute Divisions withdrew into Germany in support of their parent formations. By 21st March the Allies occupied the west bank of the Rhine, except for the section to the south between Mannheim and Karlsruhe. During the drive the US First Army seized a bridgehead across the Rhine at Remagen and the Third Army gained one at Oppenheim. The first Allied objective on the crossing of the Rhine was to encircle the rich industrial Ruhr. After a change of plan that gave Bradley's Army Group the main responsibility for the attack, the Ninth and First Armies met on 1st April at Lippstadt to complete the encirclement.

Field-Marshal Model's Army Group B, if ill-prepared for the defence of the Ruhr, settled down to fight to the last man. On 14th April the Americans cut the Ruhr pocket in two, and Model had no alternative but to surrender. The final count of prisoners exceeded 325,000, including men from the 3rd Parachute Division. 5th Parachute Division suffered a similar fate in the Nuremburg area. After the capture of the Ruhr on 18th April the general advance continued to the Elbe, while the United States Third Army struck for Vienna and the Sixth Army Group for Western Austria and the Brenner Pass.

In the East in mid-February the Russians had reached the Oder River, but they were held there for several weeks. In mid-April, after regrouping, the Russians broke through the German defences and struck for Berlin. In the south the offensive moved generally up the Danube Valley, captured Budapest and Vienna, and – with the help of Tito's partisans – cleared the Germans from most of the Balkans. The Hermann Göring Parachute Panzer Corps led by General Schmaltz was overwhelmed in East Prussia; the ambitious plans to develop an airborne armoured corps had not matured.

In Italy 1st and 4th Parachute Divisions ended their days in captivity. 10th Parachute Division joined in the battles in northern Italy, then transferred to Czechoslovakia where it surrendered to the Russians in the Prague area. Similarly, 9th Parachute Division (Bräuer), after participating briefly in the defence of Berlin, went into Russian captivity. General Student was appointed commander of Army Group Weichsel in April.

The United States First and Ninth Armies had reached the Elbe by 19th April, but they halted at that river line in accordance with prior Allied agreements. By 24th April elements of the First Belorussian front had closed a ring around Berlin. The next day the Soviet Fifth Guards Army made contact with the United States First Army at Torgau on the Elbe River south of Berlin, and Germany was split into two parts. The German Wehrmacht surrendered unconditionally on 7th May 1945.

The 'new' parachute divisions in North West Europe, no less than the earlier airborne soldiers at Eban-Emael, Holland and Crete, carried out their military duties with great skill and characteristic zeal. Lacking the special weapons and airborne training of the 'old' divisions, the 'new' *Fallschirmjäger* earned the admiration of friend and foe alike by their staunch defence of the Reich in the final catastrophic days of the war.

The achievements of German airborne forces owe much to their forceful and visionary commander, *Generaloberst* Kurt Student, who created, shaped and made the airborne arm effective. The early operations against Belgium, Holland and Crete pioneered the concept of vertical envelopment and the techniques of airborne warfare. In the defensive rôle the staunchness of the *Fallschirmjäger* in Italy, France, Russia and in the Rhineland placed these soldiers squarely in the line of German military tradition.

9 Unit Histories

7th Air Division: 22nd Air-Landing Division
1st, 2nd, 3rd, 4th, 5th, 6th, 7th, 8th, 9th, 10th Parachute Divisions
XI Air Corps: 1st and 2nd Parachute Corps: Hermann Göring (HG)
   Parachute Armoured Corps
First Parachute Army: Parachute Assault Gun Brigades XI and XII
SS Parachute Battalion 500/600

7th Air Division

Regiments: FJR 1 (3 battalions) FJR 2 (3 battalions)
         FJR 3 (3 battalions)

Commander: *Generalmajor* Student; later *Generalmajor* Putziger;
         Generalmajor Süssmann; *Generalleutnant* Petersen

   The original German airborne division formed in July 1938, still
incomplete at the outbreak of war with only two parachute regiments;
FJR 1 (*Oberst* Bräuer) and FJR 2 (*Oberst* Sturm).

1940. Only single companies took part in April in the German invasions
of Denmark and Norway. In Belgium in May, the fortress of Eban-
Emael and nearby bridges on the Albert Canal were captured in daring
raids by parachute and gliderborne sections. The assault force operated
within the command structure of General Student's *ad hoc* Air-Landing
Corps. In Holland at the same time both parachute regiments, FJR 1
and FJR 2 (two battalions only), were committed with 22nd (Air-
Landing) Division in successful raids to seize bridges, airfields and other
objectives essential to the swift military occupation of the country.
   Later in the year a third regiment, FJR 3, was raised under *Oberst*
Heidrich; also new divisional engineer, AA, MG and motorcycle units.

1941. FJR 2 (*Oberst* Sturm) was committed in April in a successful
attack on the Corinth Canal bridge in Greece. First successful
employment of airborne troops in a strategic rôle – the invasion of Crete
– followed in May. The entire division, coupled with 5th Mountain
Division under XI Air Corps, sustained very heavy casualties against
unexpectedly strong British, Commonwealth, Greek and Cretan
defences. Surviving units were posted to the Eastern front and saw
action on the Leningrad, Rzhev and Mius sectors.

1942. Committed piecemeal fashion as infantry, the division took part
in winter and summer operations on the Northern and Central sectors
in Russia. Redesignated in the late autumn as 1st Parachute Division

and withdrawn from Russia in March 1943 to the South of France.

Divisional units included artillery, medical, signals and anti-tank troops.

22nd Infantry Air-Landing (LUFTLANDE) Division

Regiments: IR 16 (3 battalions) IR 47 (3 battalions) IR 65 (3 battalions)

Commander: *Generalmajor* Graf von Sponeck; later *Generalmajor*
Wolff; *Generalmajor* Müller; *Generalmajor* Kreipe;
Generalmajor Friebe

1934-5. A normal infantry division of the first wave raised in the
Bremen-Hamburg military district (*Wehrkreis X*). Infantry Regiment 16,
in common with most infantry regiments, was redesignated in 1942 as
a Grenadier Regiment (GR).IR 16 was experimentally equipped for
air-landing operations but also retained its normal infantry equipment.

1939. IR 16 was committed in September in the Polish campaign on the
Bzura sector while the remainder of the division was stationed on the
West Wall. All withdrawn to Germany in October for fitting out and
training as an air-landing division.

1940. Under command of General Student's *ad hoc* air-landing corps,
the division (Graf von Sponeck) was committed in Northern Holland in
air-landing actions against The Hague, Rotterdam, Moerdijk and
Dordrecht, supported by elements of 7th Air Division.

1941-4. Posted in spring 1941 to Rumania on oilfield protection duty at
Ploesti and then committed on the southern sector of the Eastern front
in Eleventh Army's advance from Bukovina across the Pruth, Dniester
and Bug. Forced a Dnieper crossing at Berislav and then engaged in the
Crimea, sustaining heavy losses in the capture of Sebastopol.
Withdrawn to Greece (Salonika and Athens) for refitting as a motorised
air-landing *(Luftlande)* unit but never employed in this rôle.

A battle group (*Oberst* Bühse), comprising one company of the
motorised reconnaissance regiment and GR 47, was transported to
Tunisia in 1943. The remainder of the division was transferred to Crete
under General Kreipe. Kreipe was abducted by British commandos and
succeeded by General Friebe. The division stayed on Crete until the
island was evacuated in August 1944.

1945. Under command of XXI (Mountain) Corps, took part in operations in Montenegro against Yugoslav partisans. Surrendered there
during April 1945.

Divisional units included Artillery Regiment 22 with three light and one
heavy batteries, Reconnaissance Unit 22, Signals Unit 22, Engineer Unit
22 and Anti-Tank Unit 22.

1st Parachute Division

Regiments: FJR 1 (3 battalions) FJR 3 (3 battalions)
FJR 4 (3 battalions)

Commander: *Generalmajor* Heidrich; later (1945), *Generalmajor* Schultz

1943. Formed during early spring in the South of France, basically from 7th Air Division. Transferred to Sicily in July and engaged in operations to delay Allied forces on the Catania Plain. Defended the Primasole Bridge in a fierce engagement with British paratroops. Evacuated to the Italian mainland and engaged there in withdrawals northwards, pursued by Allied armies over the next twenty months.

1944. Heavily engaged March-May at Cassino in a distinguished defence of the Heights of Cassino and Liri Valley, key positions on the Gustav Line on the southern approaches to Rome. After the fall of Rome in June, transferred to the Adriatic front, suffering heavy losses in withdrawing to Bologna where the division put up a spirited defence of the town.

1945. Surrendered in northern Italy.

Divisional units: Artillery Regiment 1, AA 1, Engineer and Signals 1, Anti-Tank 1.

2nd Parachute Division

Regiments: FJR 2 (3 battalions) FJR 6 (3 battalions)
  FJR 7 (3 battalions)
Commander: *Generalmajor* Ramcke; later (1944), *Generalmajor* Lackner

1943. Formed in Brittany during the spring from FJR 2 (released by the former 7th Air Division) and the 4th Battalion of the former Assault Regiment and newly raised volunteer units. Transferred in the summer to the Rome area where the formation was completed. In action against Badoglio government troops and Italian *Commando Supremo* at Monte Rotondo (2nd Battalion FJR 6) after Italian capitulation in September. Gained control of Rome and later provided a force for the capture of Léros. Transferred to the Eastern front (at Zhitomir), leaving a cadre in Italy for the new 4th Parachute Division. Most of FJR 6 lost in the East; later reformed.

1944. Refitted in Germany (at Wahn) and then posted to Brittany where FJR 2 and FJR 7 surrendered in July after prolonging the defence of the port of Brest. The reformed FJR 6, attached to 91st Division in Normandy, engaged in June against Allied invasion forces. The reconstituted 2nd Division was formed in Germany and Holland under General Lackner and afterwards engaged in September in the Arnhem area and in the Reichswald. Defended the Rhine crossings in March 1945 and later surrendered in the Ruhr pocket.

Divisional units: artillery, anti-tank, AA, signals and MG units.

3rd Parachute Division

Regiments: FJR 5 (3 battalions) FJR 8 (3 battalions)
  FJR 9 (3 battalions)
Commander: *Generalmajor* Schimpf

1943-4. Formed during autumn 1943 in the Reims area of France with a nucleus of experienced Luftwaffe personnel and 3rd Battalion FJR 1. After training in northern France posted to Brittany, then to Normandy where in June 1944 the division was engaged during the Allied landings. Suffered heavy losses at St Lô. Overwhelmed in the Falaise pocket in July. The divisional commander escaped, though wounded.

Reformed at Oldenzaal in Holland during October 1944, largely from Luftwaffe ground personnel of *Flieger* Regiments 22, 51 and 53.

Transferred to the Eifel area in West Germany in readiness for the Ardennes counter-offensive in December; played an important part in support of the Panzer divisions in their abortive attempt to reach Antwerp.

1945. Engaged in the Eifel area. Withdrew over the Rhine. Located in the Remagen area, then in the Ruhr. Surrendered with German Army Group B in Ruhr pocket.

Divisional units: artillery, anti-tank, engineer, heavy mortar and signals units.

4th Parachute Division

Regiments: FJR 10 (3 battalions) FJR 11 (3 battalions)
          FJR 12 (3 battalions)
Commander: *Generalmajor* Trettner

1943-5. Formed in Italy at Perugia during late autumn 1943 from cadres provided by 2nd Parachute Division and members of the Italian *Folgore* and *Nembo* Divisions. Completed in the Anzio area in January 1944 where the divisions under command of 1st (Parachute) Corps engaged the Allied landings. From then on continuously engaged in Italy, suffering heavy losses in defensive battles north of Florence and later at Rimini and Bologna. Surrendered in northern Italy to US forces in the Bozen area.

Divisional units: Artillery Regiment 4, Anti-Tank Battalion 4, AA 4, Engineer 4, Signals 4.

5th Parachute Division

Regiments: FJR 13 (3 battalions) FJR 14 (3 battalions)
          FJR 15 (3 battalions)
Commander: *Generalmajor* Wilke; later (1942), *Generalmajor* Heilmann

1943-4. Formed during March 1943 in the Reims area of France from the Demonstration Battalion *(Lehrbatallion)* of XI Air Corps and the 3rd Battalions of FJR 3 and FJR 4. Posted to Brittany for training, then to Normandy where the division was engaged during the Allied landings in June 1944. Virtually destroyed in the Falaise pocket.

Reformed under General Ludwig Heilmann in Germany and Holland from Luftwaffe ground personnel, a shadow of its former self; the new division took part in the Ardennes counter-offensive of late December 1944.

1945. Withdrew in a series of delaying actions into central Germany, ending in captivity near Nürburgring or in the Ruhr in March 1945.

Divisional units: Artillery Regiment 5, AA 5, Engineer Battalion 5, Signals 5, Heavy Mortar 5, Anti-Tank 5.

6th Parachute Division

Regiments: FJR 16 (3 battalions) FJR 17 (3 battalions)
FJR 18 (3 battalions)
Commander: *Generalmajor* Plocher

1944-5. Formed during June 1944 in the Amiens area of northern France. The division suffered heavy losses in operations to hold back the Allies after their Normandy breakout in July. During this time FJR 16 and staff were flown to East Prussia and redesignated as *Fallschirm-Grenadier Regiment 3* of the Hermann Göring Panzer Corps. Surviving battle groups formed the nucleus of 7th Parachute Division; the remainder reformed in Holland and were engaged in the Arnhem area in September 1944 and later in the Rhineland battles. Surrendered to American forces in April 1945 near Zutphen.

Divisional units: Artillery Regiment 6, Anti-Tank 6, AA 6, Engineer 6, Heavy Mortar 6.

7th Parachute Division

Regiments: FJR 19 (3 battalions) FJR 20 (3 battalions)
FJR 21 (3 battalions)
Commander: *Generalmajor* Erdmann

1944-5. Formed during October 1944 at Venlo in Lower Holland from *Division Erdmann* (raised in the Bitsch area of Alsace during September) with personnel from the *Fallschirm-Waffen* school and battle groups of 6th Parachute Division. Assembled under the command of 2nd Parachute Corps (Meindl).

Engaged during February 1945 in the Reichswald defensive battles against British 3rd and 51st Infantry Divisions of 30th Corps, destroying large numbers of tanks in a noteworthy action at Kappeln. In March, after vigorously contesting the Allied Rhine crossings, withdrew into North West Germany, surrendering in the Oldenburg area to British forces in April 1945.

Divisional units: Artillery Regiment 7, Anti-Tank 7, AA 7, Engineer 7, Signals 7.

8th Parachute Division

Regiments: FJR 22 (3 battalions) FJR 23 (projected)
FJR 24 (3 battalions)
Commander: *Generalmajor* Wadehn

1944-5. Formed during December 1944 in Cologne-Wahn area of Germany. Under the command of Meindl's 2nd Parachute Corps was engaged during February 1945 in the defensive Reichswald battles. The division scored noteworthy successes in delaying actions against British and Canadian units of 21st Army Group. Withdrew into North West Germany and, after fiercely contesting the Allied advance south of Bremen, surrendered in that area in April 1945.

Divisional units included Engineers 8, Signals 8

9th Parachute Division

Regiments: FJR 25 (3 battalions) FJR 26 (2 battalions)
FJR 27 (incomplete)
Commander: *Generalmajor* Bräuer

1944-5. Formed during December 1944 from mixed Luftwaffe personnel. Stationed (partly) during February 1945 in defence of Berlin and (partly - two battalions) in the defence of the beleagured fortress town of Breslau (under General Niehoff). Surrendered to Soviet forces during May 1945.

Divisional units: Artillery Regiment 9, Engineer Battalion 9, Heavy mortar 9, Signals 9, Anti-Tank 9.

10th Parachute Division

Regiments: FJR 28 (3 battalions) FJR 29 (3 battalions)
FJR 30 (3 battalions)
Commander: *Generalmajor* von Hofmann

1945. Formed during March 1945 from detachments of 1st and 4th Parachute Divisions in the Krems-Melk area of Austria. FJR 30 engaged by Soviets in Steirmark at St Pölten in the Danube valley. Transferred to Moravia in the area southeast of Prague where the division surrendered to the Russians, along with First Panzer Army and twenty-nine other divisions, in May 1945.

Divisional units: Artillery Regiment 10 (incomplete), Engineer Battalion 10, Signals Battalion 10.

XI Air (Flieger) Corps

Commander: *Generalleutnant* Kurt Student

1940. Formed from the *ad hoc* Air-Landing Corps (in control of 7th Air and 22nd Air-Landing Divisions) during summer 1940 to control the expansion of airborne units.

1941. Under the command of 4th Air Fleet (Löhr) controlled 7th Air and 5th Mountain Divisions in the attack on Crete, Operation 'Mercury'.

1942. Continuously responsible for planning airborne operations; also training and development of weapons and equipment.

Early 1943. Assigned to OKW reserve and stationed at Nîmes in southern France. In control of 1st and 2nd Parachute Divisions. During April transferred to Rome in control of 2nd Parachute Division and 29th Panzer Grenadier Division; responsible for the Rome *coup* and freeing Mussolini 12th September 1943.

1944. During March upgraded to 1st Parachute Army and located at Nancy in east central France.

Corps troops: Assault (Air-Landing) Regiment, Demonstration Battalion, AA MG Battalion, Reconnaissance, Signals, Medical and Engineer units.

Other units responsible to XI Air Corps during 1943 included the Italian *Folgore* Regiment with German officers and under-officers.

1st Parachute Corps

Commander: *Generalleutant* Schlemm, later *Generalleutnant* Heidrich

1944. Formed in January in central Italy to control 4th Parachute Division and 3rd Panzer Grenadier Division (Fourteenth Army) in the Anzio-Nettuno battle zone. Henceforth continuously engaged in the Italian theatre with either or both 1st and 4th Parachute Divisions under command.

1945. Withdrew into Upper Italy under pressure from Allied armies, conducting strong rearguard actions north of Florence. Surrendered to the Allies in April 1945.

Corps troops: Corps Artillery Regiment 11, AR Assault Gun Brigade 11, AA Regiment 11, MG Battalion 11, Reconnaissance and Signals Battalions 11, Heavy Mortar Battalion 11.

2nd Parachute Corps

Commander: *Generalleutnant* Meindl

Late 1943. Formed in eastern France by conversion of XIII Air Corps Headquarters, formerly Division Meindl; after that the corps' task of raising Luftwaffe field divisions had been fulfilled. Raised two new parachute divisions: 3rd (Schimpf) and 5th (Wilke).

1944. During early summer under command of German Seventh Army in Normandy and assumed operational task of containing US 7th Corps (Collins) and 19th Corps (Corlett) in their beachhead positions (Omaha and Utah). Later, with the Panzer Corps and other Seventh Army units encircled in the Falaise pocket. Both parachute divisions were destroyed, the Corps commander only narrowly escaping capture.

1945. Under command of First Parachute Army (Schlemm) after reforming in Holland during previous autumn. In control of 7th (Erdmann) and 8th (Wadehn) Parachute Divisions. Performed notably in the Reichswald battles against British 21st Army Group and in defence of German 'bridgeheads' on the left bank of the Rhine.

Corps troops: Artillery Regiment 12, Assault Gun Brigade 12, AA Regiment 12, MG Battalion 12, Signals Battalion 12, Reconnaissance Battalion 12.

Hermann Göring Parachute Armoured Corps (Fallschirm Panzer Korps)

Commander: *Generalleutnant* Schmalz

1944-5. This corps was in control of a Panzer division (HG 1) and a Panzer Grenadier division (HG 2) and made its appearance in East Prussia in October 1944. During its short life the corps operated in a straightforward defensive rôle until swept into oblivion in the wake of the Soviet offensive in January 1945. Neither division was employed on airborne operations but this rôle was envisaged earlier (in 1942) when experiments in cooperation between armoured and airborne units were conducted by the Hermann Göring Brigade.

The Hermann Göring Brigade was committed in Tunisia in 1943 and partly destroyed there. The Brigade was reformed in Sicily in July as a Panzer Grenadier division under General Conrath. After conversion soon afterwards to a full Panzer division was engaged the following year by the Soviets in the Warsaw area. The division (HG 1) coupled with a new Panzer Grenadier division (HG 2) was then built into the Hermann Göring *Fallschirm Panzer Korps*.

Corps troops included AA Regiment HG, Engineer Battalion HG, Corps Signals, Medical, Supply and other units.

First Parachute Army

Commander: *Generaloberst* Student; later (November 1944), *Generaloberst* Schlemm; (March 1945), *Generaloberst* Blumentritt; (10th April 1945), *Generaloberst* Student; (28th April 1945), *Generaloberst* Straube

1944-5. Formed during March 1944 under General Student by upgrading XI Air (*Flieger*) Corps in eastern France. Responsible for raising and training new parachute divisions for Western Europe and resupplying parachute forces in Italy and Russia. Operational in June, 2nd Corps was committed in Normandy but after the Allied breakthrough to the Seine First Parachute Army occupied defensive positions in Belgium and eastern Holland.

First Parachute Army was in direct control of 2nd Corps and two infantry and a rather weak Panzer Corps formation, which included the reconstituted Panzer *Lehrdivision*. After Field-Marshal Montgomery's forces overran Belgium, First Parachute Army consolidated on the Maas and Lower Rhine under Army Group H. Severely engaged commencing 17th September by Operation Market Garden, Student's paratroopers, coupled with Twenty-Fifth Army, suffered heavy losses at the hands of the American 82nd and 101st Airborne Divisions and the advancing British 30th Corps around Eindhoven and Nijmegen. *Generaloberst* Student now appointed to command Army Group H.

During November and December 1944 and the early months of 1945, First Parachute Army under *Generaloberst* Schlemm imposed unexpected delays on Allied offensive operations mounted towards the Rhine river barrier. Resisting pressure from six British and Canadian army corps, Army Group H protected the withdrawal of German army units from West Rhineland districts, in an area where there were no fewer than nine road and rail crossings. The allies were thus denied a Rhine crossing until, further south, the Remagen bridge fell intact into American hands in March. The east bank of the Rhine was effectively held until two Allied airborne divisions landed beyond the river on 23-24 March and opened the way for the advance of the Allied armies to the Elbe.

An orderly withdrawal was carried out by First Parachute Army (now Blumentritt) in the direction of Hamburg and surrender followed in April 1945 in the Oldenburg area.

142

Army troops included an 'assault' battalion, Panzer Regiment 21, Heavy Mortar Battalion 21, Engineer Regiment 21 (3 battalions), Signals Regiment 21, but full details are lacking. Many other administrative units and schools were responsible to the Parachute Army HQ.

Parachute Assault Gun Brigade XI (Green Devils Brigade)

Early 1944. Raised in Germany from *Fallschirmjäger* volunteers. After training and fitting out in France, engaged in the fighting around Nancy and there practically destroyed.

Late 1944. Refitted in November in support of 5th Parachute Division. Engaged by the US 4th Armoured Division in the Ardennes and there again practically destroyed.

May 1945. Surrendered to the Russians.

Parachute Assault Gun Brigade XII

Raised concurrrently with XI Brigade from volunteers.

Early 1944. Posted to France for fitting out.

Mid-1944. Engaged in June south of St Lô against invasion forces in support of 3rd Parachute Division and almost totally destroyed with that division in the Falaise pocket.

Autumn 1944. Refitted in September in support of 7th Parachute Division (Erdmann) and engaged in the Reichswald battles in early 1945 (First Parachute Army). After continuous action surrendered to the Allies at Wilhemshaven in May 1945. The brigade was credited with the destruction of 260 Allied tanks. (See biography of *Leutnant* Deutsch.)

SS Parachute Battalion 500/600

Commander: SS *Hauptsturmführer* Rybka

1943. Raised by the *Waffen*-SS Command in the autumn for special security missions. Officers joined as volunteers from other SS units on the authority of a secret command order (*G-Kommando*). Half of the men came to the originally designated 500 Battalion as volunteers, but the remainder were taken from military penal camps. Parachute training was given at Kraljevo in Yugoslavia.

1944. Parachute school transferred to Papa in Hungary. The first parachute operation was mounted on Whit Sunday against Marshal Tito's mountain headquarters at Drvar, Bosnia. Tito and staff escaped and battalion reduced to about 200 men in a three day long battle with partisans. The battalion was reconstituted but made up with only twenty per cent penal troops.

Acted in a corps rearguard action in Kurland in August when the Russians first broke through to the Baltic. On 14th October the battalion was transferred from the Führer's direction to Skorzeny's overall command. Posted to the neighbourhood of Vienna, the battalion was earmarked but not used for a parachute operation against the Burg in Budapest as part of Skorzeny's *coup* in anticipation of the fall of Admiral Horthy.

The renamed 600 Battalion was reinforced by first-class experienced troops from army units stationed in Lower Saxony and Westphalia; the penal conscripts being pardoned and reinstated in their former ranks.

In the Ardennes offensive the battalion operated under Skorzeny's Special SS Brigade and infiltrated the Allied lines in American uniforms. The mission was not a success and Germans taken prisoner in American uniforms were executed. Despite this, havoc was temporarily created across American lines of communication.

1945. In the middle of January the remains of the battalion was gathered together again at Neu-Strelitz and thrown into a bridgehead at Schwedt on the Oder. The bridgehead was not evacuated until 26th February and then only on orders from a higher command. On 9th March an assault action took place at another small bridgehead on the Oder near Zehnden. Reinforcing a regiment of marine infantry, 600 Battalion succeeded in extending the bridgehead but the lack of heavy weapons prevented the possibility of a breakthrough in the area. Between 25th-27th March the Russians sent an armoured brigade, two infantry brigades and an assorted cavalry division supported by 500 guns against the small bridgehead.

600 Battalion with the SS Assault Section 501 had been decimated by the Oder battles, but was reinforced again at Oderberg. From 20th April the battalion acted as 'fire brigade' along the Oder: at first in flank skirmishes against Russian tanks at Bernau, then at Eberswalde-Finowfurt; and finally fought rearguard actions in the westward withdrawal at Prenzlau and Neu-Ruppin. Faced with surrender to the Russians at Neu-Ruppin, the 180 survivors of 600 Battalion made their way to Hagenow where they surrendered to the Americans.

10 Personalities

STUDENT Kurt *Generaloberst*

Knight's Cross with Oak Leaves
Golden Flying Award with Diamonds

Kurt Student was born on 12th May 1890 at Birkholz near Neumark in Brandenburg. As was customary for Prussian landowning families, young Student was sent along with his four brothers to an Imperial military cadet school. Thus at the age of eleven he was subjected to the harsh discipline of a Prussian military preparatory school. After Potsdam he commenced his secondary education at a senior cadet school (*Hauptkadettenanstalt*) at Lichterfelde.

On graduation he went in 1909 as a potential officer 'on probation' to a *Jäger* battalion of his own choice, *Graf York von Wartenburg*. Sent the following year to the War School in Danzig, *Fähnrich* Student was formally commissioned into his regiment in 1911, and posted as a subaltern to the 1st Battalion at Ortelsburg.

In 1913 *Leutnant* Student volunteered for flying in the hope that his application would not be taken seriously. Much to his surprise he was accepted for flying training at the home of German aviation at Johannisthal near Berlin, and was awarded a pilot's certificate in the autumn of the same year.

With the outbreak of hostilities in 1914 he flew to the Eastern Front in an Albatros plane and was promoted *Oberleutnant*. After Tannenberg and Augustovo Student joined a small team of pilots specially selected to try out new Fokker planes fitted with machine-guns. On his first test combat sortie he engaged four Russian planes and shot down a Morane.

In the autumn of 1915 XVIII Corps was transferred to the Western Front. In the following July the Germans formed the *Jagdwaffe*, a new air arm consisting of pursuit squadrons. The new combat squadrons, popularly known as '*Jasta*' received all the latest equipment. *Jasta 9* was equipped with Fokker biplanes and assembled on the central sector in Champagne under its young *Staffelführer* or squadron-leader, *Hauptmann* Student. *Jasta 9* was employed in Champagne until the end of the war. In late 1917 the now veteran pilot earned convalescent leave after being severely wounded in the left shoulder in personal combat with a French air ace. Kurt Student survived the war in the rank of captain.

With the demise of the Imperial army, the *Reichswehr* that emerged from the conference tables at Versailles was limited to 100,000 men. Hans von Seekt, an able general of the old school, who commanded the now small but professional army, planned an efficient force, which was capable of rapid expansion at the first favourable opportunity.

Student's appointment in 1920 to the Central Flying Office (*Fliegerzentrale*) was concerned with the technological aspects of equipping a non-existent German Air Force. German airmen indulged their passion for flying at this time in gliders and Student's career at the *Fliegerzentrale* was temporarily interrupted after fracturing his skull in a glider crash in the winter of 1921. As a director in charge of air technology, in 1923 he visited the German air force mission training secretly with Russian airmen at Lipetsk near Voronezh in the Soviet Union.

In 1928 *Hauptmann* Student reverted to the infantry: in peace-time armies promotion for career-officers is slow, and opportunities for field command fiercely competitive. Accordingly the soldier-airman was posted to a distinguished old regiment, *Infanterie-Regiment 2*, stationed at Lötzen, and in 1929 was promoted battalion commander in the rank of major.

Major Student terminated his tour of duty with 2nd Infantry Regiment in the winter of 1932, and was re-assigned as Director of Air Technical Training Schools. With the advent of Chancellor Hitler in January 1933, plans for the immediate expansion of German armed forces were scarcely delayed. The army and navy were to be more than doubled in strength: the new Luftwaffe, in the hands of the senior aviator Hermann Göring, was to comprise a nucleus of 1,000 planes. Promoted in November 1933 to *Oberstleutnant,* Student was now completely engrossed in arranging an ever-increasing number of technical courses for airmen.

Hitler overtly rejected the conditions of the Versailles Treaty in 1935, but several years were needed before the Luftwaffe would rank as an efficient, fighting air arm. Now a full colonel, *Oberst* Student's work embraced all aspects of airplane technology, equipment, weaponry and parachutes. He travelled widely in the mid-1930's visiting foreign military manoeuvres, factories and workshops, and made an appreciative evaluation of the Russian parachute drops as part of the Soviet exercises near Kiev in 1935. And his next appointment as Inspector of Flying Schools brought him into contact with the first German parachute training school at Stendal two years later.

In June 1938 his command of the 7th Air Division shortly to be formed at Münster was confirmed in the rank of major-general. *Generalmajor* Student had been given a free hand to build up the newest kind of formation in the German armed services. Whilst actively developing a policy for the new sky battalions; Student rigidly enforced the highest standards of training at the parachute school at Stendal. As trained *Fallschirmjäger* arrived to reinforce the original parachute battalion and army company that existed in 1938, so the ambitious concept of a parachute division developed into practical reality.

After the 7th Air Division's sortie into Moravia following the annexation of the Sudetenland, OKW approved the establishment of two separate airborne divisions. The 7th Air Division was designated a paratroop formation and the 22nd Infantry Division assigned to the air-landing rôle. *Generalmajor* Student was now given the title of Inspector Airborne Forces but retained command of the 7th Air Division.

Whilst the Panzer columns and dive bombers delivered the *coup de grâce* in Poland in September 1939, the commitment of the Air Division near Jaroslav on the River San was later pronounced unnecessary by the Army High Command. Student himself narrowly escaped capture when his staff car strayed into a Polish defensive position. Hitler was positively anxious however to use airborne forces for the projected invasions of France and the Low Countries.

Relatively unimportant drops were first made by a parachute battalion in April 1940 at Aalborg and Vordingborg in Denmark and Stavanger and Dombas (via Oslo) in Norway. On 10th May seven, gliders were landed inside the walls of Eban-Emael in Belgium while parachutists nearby secured vital crossings of the Albert canal and Meuse river. The main ground forces reached Eban-Emael in the early hours of the following day.

At the same time the *ad hoc* airborne corps had encountered brave Dutch resistance in the areas of The Hague and Rotterdam. Student (now *Generalleutnant*) personally commanded the 7th Air Division dropped near Rotterdam. The Dutch capitulated on the afternoon of 14th May. German casualties amounted to 180 officers and men killed and wounded; Student himself being hit in the head by a sniper's bullet in Rotterdam.

Whilst the airborne battalions were inundated with praise from the Führer, their commander underwent a series of serious operations at a clinic in Berlin. He owed his life to the skill of a Dutch surgeon first operating in bomb-ravaged Rotterdam.

When *Generalleutnant* Student returned to duty in September 1940, the airborne corps had achieved the status of *corps d'élite* not only in the eyes of the Luftwaffe but in those of the Army as well. Warned that he must not parachute or travel in a glider, he settled down at once to his immense administrative duties as new recruits and equipment began to pour in. *Fliegerkorps XI* had already been formally established.

Student now gave consideration to operational plans for the capture of Gibraltar, the Cape Verde islands, Malta and certain of the Greek islands. Student showed no special interest in the commitment of his men for the putative invasion of the south coast of England. The 7th Air Division moved into Bulgaria in the winter of 1940 in preparation for the invasion of Greece. The 22nd Division was flown into Rumania.

When Hitler launched his invasion of Yugoslavia and simultaneously entered Greece on 6th April 1941, a definite policy for the deployment of XI Air Corps in the Mediterranean battle zone had not been adopted. Student fixed the focus of his attention on Cyprus and Crete, but the capture of the latter offered the greatest strategic advantages for the conduct of the war in the Mediterranean as well as the Balkan theatres. In late April Hitler accepted the plans to seize the Corinth isthmus and the island of Crete. A strong force was landed by parachute and glider at the Corinth bridge towards the end of the month in an attempt to cut off Allied forces in process of hasty withdrawal from the Greek mainland.

Student flew to Athens to establish his headquarters for the Cretan operation in the Hotel Grande-Bretagne. Seven airfields in southern Greece were chosen for emplaning the airborne corps and its *matériel* for the 200-or so- mile flight to Crete. Rather than land in one place *Generalleutnant* Student favoured the dispersal of his dropping zones along the northern littoral of Crete. As part of the first lift Máleme on the western sector was to be seized by Meindl's Assault Regiment landing simultaneously with the right of Süssmann's centre group at Canea. The second lift was destined for Retimo and Herakleion carrying the left of Süssmann's group to Retimo and Bräuer's regimental group to Herakleion. A third lift was intended to reinforce the three main battle zones. Bräuer was to hold out in the Herakleion area until the arrival of Ringel's 5th Mountain Division by seaborne invasion on to the eastern sector. The Mountain Division was to take the place of the 22nd Division which was stranded in Rumania.

Assessments of the strength of Freyberg's Allied garrison varied and the morale of his troops was under-estimated. Following intensive bombardment the paratroops struck on the morning of 20th May . Although chaos reigned on the Greek airfields as the Ju 52's were turned round for successive lifts, 8,000 troops were on the ground in Crete by the late afternoon. But at nightfall in Athens signals radioed through a rear link manned in the Máleme area forced Student to alter his tactical thinking. Nearly 2,000 of the troops on the western sector were dead or wounded, Meindl was seriously wounded and Süssmann was dead. Many of his forces had landed well off target and the important airfield at Retimo had not been taken.

Generalleutnant Student decided to concentrate on the neighbourhood of Máleme and drive eastwards along the coast. Ringel's Division was reassigned for air-landing at Máleme. Impetus was given to the advance when it was discovered that New Zealand troops had vacated defensive positions at

Máleme. As German casualties mounted so reinforcements were sent in and units holding out along the line were re-supplied with ammunition and rations. After the fall of Canea Student flew in from Athens and was visibly shaken by the heavy casualties. Suda Bay, Retimo and Herakleion fell and the Allied evacuation was completed by the end of the month. About 6,000 German troops were dead and nearly 4,000 of these casualties were airborne men.

When Student went to Hitler's headquarters at Wolfschanze two months later he did so with mixed emotions, but the heavy losses in Crete had not shaken his belief in the airborne concept. Awarding Student the Knight's Cross, the Führer gave due acknowledgement to XI Air Corps' victory in battle, but argued that strategically and tactically the island of Crete was a case on its own. In future the Allies would be too well prepared: the cost of the Cretan adventure was too great; the paratrooper had had his day.

XI Air Corps returned to Germany and the 7th Air Division was posted in the ground rôle to Russia. With growing reports of Allied interest in parachute formations, Student pleaded with Hitler to reconsider his views on the employment of the airborne corps. Under the protection of Göring the strength of the parachute force was considerably increased, but its true rôle on large scale operations was forever denied to its resourceful commander.

Generalfeldmarschall Rommel's triumph in the desert in the autumn of 1941 called for sound logistic support. The island of Malta presented a threat to the Axis supply lines to North Africa as well as providing a vital link in the British Mediterranean supply route to Egypt. Student turned enthusiastically to an operational study for an airborne attack on Malta. 7th Air Division was to be partnered by the Italian *Folgore* Division. The corps assisted by an air-landed division was to be under the overall command of the Prince of Piedmont. The landing scheduled for June 1942 was never attempted: the *Folgore* Division departed for the desert as did Ramcke's Brigade from 7th Air Division. What was left of the 7th was sent to Normandy and thence to Russia. As a consolation prize Student hatched a plot for a drop on Gibraltar.

The new 2nd Parachute Division was stationed in Brittany. In May 1943 XI Air Corps, with the 1st (7th) and 2nd Divisions, was earmarked for the defence of Italy. In July the 1st Parachute Division was to see the Cretan assault re-enacted by British and American parachute and glider forces in Sicily. With the removal of the Duce from the seat of power and the Italian capitulation in the same month, Hitler discussed plans for a pro-Fascist *coup* in Rome. *Generalleutnant* Student's corps was chosen to hold Rome, overthrow the new government and restore Mussolini to power and block the advance of Allied forces who were expected to land in the south. The rescue of Mussolini was assigned to SS-*Obersturmbannführer* Otto Skorzeny.

Mussolini had been taken from his first place of confinement on the island of Ponza to a mountain hide-out on the Gran Sasso plateau. Skorzeny's ingenious plans for plucking the Duce from the Hotel Albergo-Rifugio were submitted to Student who finally agreed to a glider landing on the high ground beside the hotel. On 12th September Student set up his control centre at an airfield near Rome while Skorzeny's twelve DFS 230 gliders crammed with Luftwaffe and *Waffen*-SS paratroopers were towed to the Gran Sasso. With a battalion under *Major* Mors lodged at the end of the roadway that led to the funicular, eight of the gliders sailed on to the car park inside the hotel grounds. Mussolini was taken off with Skorzeny in Student's personal Fieseler Storch piloted by *Hauptmann* Gerlach to the control centre whence he was transferred by Heinkel 111 to Vienna.

XI Air Corps was inevitably broken up. The 2nd Parachute Division was ordered to the Russian front and the new 4th Parachute Division raised for the Italian theatre. Targets for parachute landings were chosen on the islands of

Kos, Léros and Samos in the Dodecanese. Throughout the winter and spring of 1943-44 paratroopers braced the German defensive lines on the Garigliano and Sangro rivers, at the Cassino stronghold and were also thrown against the bridgehead at Anzio.

In March 1944 the Parachute High Command was set up at Nancy in northern France. *Generalleutnant* Student's task was to raise a new airborne force and in addition to keep his divisions in Russia and Italy supplied with replacements. With *Fallschirmkorps I* fighting on in Italy until the end of the war, *Fallschirmkorps II* was raised from the new recruits passing through the parachute training schools in France and Germany. In June 1944 when the Allies landed on the Normandy beaches Student commanded a complete parachute army (*Fallschirm Armee*); and Meindl's 2nd Corps was committed in July to the first major counter-attack of the Normandy campaign.

During July 1944 Student's headquarters was removed to Berlin where chaos reigned as a result of the attempt to kill Hitler at Rastenburg. When the Allied armies broke out from Normandy to the Seine, Student was ordered to assemble all available paratroop regiments and build a defensive position in the region of the Albert Canal in Belgium under Army Group B.

Field-Marshal Model's Army Group B made an accurate assessment of the line of advance of Dempsey's British Second Army into Holland. When on 17th September Allied airborne troops descended from the sky at Eindhoven, Nijmegen and Arnhem hopefully to secure the river crossings necessary for a swift Allied advance beyond the Rhine, *Generaloberst* Student was situated in a house within sight of the Eindhoven and Nijmegen dropping zones. He was so impressed by the sight of the sky armada that he did not at first awaken to the dangers of the situation; but by mid-afternoon the plans for Operation 'Market Garden', taken from a dead American, were on his desk.

Whilst SS-*Panzerkorps II* was to wipe out the *logement* effected in the north by the British 1st Airborne Division at Arnhem, Student's First Parachute Army stood astride the main highway (Hell's Highway) from Eindhoven to Nijmegen and Arnhem in the path of the Second Army. Always under intense air and artillery bombardment and the pressure principally of British units across the Wilhelmina canal towards the Maas and Waal rivers, the First Parachute Army was brought near to breaking point.

On 1st November 1944 *Generaloberst* Student was named Commander of the new Army Group H. Army Group H, which was to comprise the First Parachute Army and the new Twenty-Fifth Army, was to block the Allied approach march to the Rhine. Student's representations to the High Command for the reinforcements and equipment needed to defend the Rhine incurred disfavour with the Führer. He was removed from his post in favour of von Blaskowitz; only to be reinstated for an abortive counter-offensive against the Allied Rhine bridgehead in March 1945. Student was then directed to return to the headquarters of the Parachute High Command.

Germany was being invaded from both west and east. As the Russians poured across the Oder only emaciated German divisions augmented by *Volkssturm* and armed youths stood in the path of the Soviet tanks storming onwards to Berlin. In mid-April Student flew to Mecklenburg to take over Heinrici's Army Group falling back in disorder from the Oder. As Student's Heinkel 111 approached the run-way the plane was greeted by a hail of Russian machine-gun fire and was obliged to turn back for Lübeck. When the British army reached Schleswig-Holstein, *Generaloberst* Student was taken prisoner.

In the inter-war years the chaos that reigned in the Weimar Republic was replaced in 1933 by a new social order. Hitler's Third Reich did indeed bring new political and social order to the home scene, and promptly sought to export the Nazi philosophy by means of renewed Prussian military efficiency with frenetic zeal. Student was in the forefront of developments in military aviation during those portentous times. But his concept of airborne assault fully tested in the harsh reality of the Battle of Crete in 1941 was never in the mainstream of German military thinking. The mighty Panzers occupied pride of place. At noon on 17th September 1944 as Brereton's Allied Airborne Army descended from the sky over Holland, *Generaloberst* Student must have reflected that as actor-dramatist he had been denied a starring rôle in his own play.

HEIDRICH Richard *Generalleutnant*

Richard Heidrich was born on 28th July 1896 and died in the Bergedorf hospital in Hamburg on 23rd December 1947. In the First World War he volunteered for the infantry and returned home as a regimental adjutant. After service with the *Freikorps* in Lithuania, Heidrich joined the *Reichswehr* and shortly earned a staff course at the War Academy.

In 1936 he volunteered for the original parachute infantry company and completed six jumps at Stendal. The company grew and *Major* Heidrich was promoted battalion commander. He was assigned to the staff of 7th Air Division as early as January 1939; but after some disagreement with his colleagues, Heidrich returned to the army for the French invasion as a regimental commander. Later in 1940 *Oberst* Heidrich was confirmed in the appointment of Commander of FJR 3.

In Crete Heidrich's regiment was dropped south of Retimo in the area of Galatas where FJR 3 was surrounded and heavily engaged from every direction until relieved by forces arriving from the west. *Oberst* Heidrich next saw action with 7th Air Division on the Russian front where FJR 3 is particularly associated with the Battle of Leningrad.

Returning to the west *Generalmajor* Heidrich went as divisional commander of the renamed 1st Parachute Division to the Mediterranean theatre. Here his division was thrown into the Battle of Sicily and he reached the apogee of his career amongst the devastated heights of Monte Cassino. The British attributed Churchillian qualities of leadership to the resolute German paratroop commander at this time. He commanded 1st Parachute Corps which surrendered to the Allies in Italy in April 1945.

Heidrich was an exceptional general who demanded and freely received the utmost loyalty from his men. Character and achievement counted a great deal with Richard Heidrich, and he was held in special esteem by the men of FJR 3. His last instructions in impending battle were: 'Keep together and don't forget the dead and those you left behind at home.'

MEINDL Eugen *Generalleutnant*

Knight's Cross with Oak Leaves

Eugen Meindl was born on 16th July 1892 at Donnaueschingen near Lake Constance. Meindl joined the 67th Field Artillery Regiment at twenty years of age as a potential officer (*Fahnenjunker*). Commissioned into the regiment he went through the First World War successively as platoon commander, battery commander and adjutant.

In 1921 Meindl joined the *Reichswehr* and continued to serve in the new German army formed under Adolf Hitler. After the annexation of Austria he was appointed to the command of 112th Mountain Artillery Regiment based at Graz.

Oberst Meindl first met the paratroopers at Narvik in 1940. Operating with the German mountain troops he was dropped with the parachute party in the area without any prior training. His transfer to airborne forces was only a matter of time. His Assault Regiment contributed a decisive share to the conquest of the Máleme sector in Crete.

He fought in Russia in the winter of 1941-42 in command of Battle Group Meindl, first on the central sector and later south of Lake Il'men. As *Generalmajor* he assembled Luftwaffe field units into Division Meindl for service on the northern sector. His experience with the air force infantry regiments led to his raising twenty-two new Luftwaffe field divisions as Corps commander of *Fliegerkorps XIII*.

Generalleutnant Meindl's 2nd Parachute Corps was formed from the staff of XIII Air Corps in late 1943 in Eastern France and two parachute divisions (3rd and 5th) were committed at the Normandy beachhead in June 1944. Meindl's Corps assumed the operational task of containing the United States 7th Corps (Collins) and 19th Corps (Corlett) advancing from Utah and Omaha beaches. The Americans were fiercely counterattacked along the oblique line St Mere-Eglise – Carentan – St Lô. Forced eastwards Meindl's two parachute divisions were trapped by British and Canadian troops in the vicinity of Falaise.

The 2nd Parachute Corps was virtually destroyed; *Generalleutnant* Meindl himself only narrowly escaping capture before the Argentan – Falaise gap was closed.

Regrouped under First Parachute Army for the defence of Belgium and Holland, Meindl's corps fought until the end at Oldenburg in April 1945. After the German capitulation Eugen Meindl was held in captivity by the Allies until September 1945. He died six years later on 24th January 1951 and is buried at his birthplace at Donnaueschingen.

RAMCKE Hermann Bernard *Generalmajor*

Knight's Cross with Oak Leaves, Swords and Diamonds

Hermann Ramcke was born on 24th January 1889 in North Germany and died on 4th July 1968. As a boy he went to sea under sail and enlisted as a marine infantry soldier in the First World War. Decorated in Flanders, Ramcke was one of the few German soldiers to be commissioned from the ranks during the course of the war. During 1918-19 he served on in the 'freedom struggle' in the Baltic States.

'Hermann Bernard' or 'Papa Ramcke', Ramcke's more familiar names, went to the Second World War with the army in Poland in a rôle that was not entirely to his liking. In the summer of 1940 he volunteered for parachute training school. The mandatory six jumps to qualify for wings were normally extended over a period of six days and no exceptions were allowed even for senior officers. Ramcke, who was then fifty-one years of age, completed his six jumps in three days, two on each day.

Serving first in Heidrich's FJR 3, a period of reserve units and war schools followed before the invasion of Crete. *Oberst* Ramcke, who was dropped at Máleme on 21st May, took over West Group after Meindl was seriously wounded. The reinforced West Group captured Máleme airfield after a day of bitter fighting.

Awarded the Knight's Cross in Crete, *Generalmajor* Ramcke was assigned as chief instructor to the Italian *Folgore* Division and was involved in the plan to seize Malta. When the operation did not materialize the Ramcke brigade was despatched to the desert. In late October 1941 the brigade lay back in the area of the Qattara depression during the withdrawal of German forces from El Alamein. The brigade's own escape was effected through British-held territory over a distance of 185 miles with the help of the vehicles belonging to a captured British supply column.

The 2nd Parachute Division was formed in France in the spring of 1943 under *Generalmajor* Ramcke. In the summer the division was thrown in as part of the airborne corps *coup d'état* in Rome. Transferred the same year to the Russian front, Ramcke and his men fought at Zhitomir, Kirovograd and other locations in the Ukraine.

Finally for Ramcke came the battle for the Brest fortress in September 1944. After the Normandy deadlock had been resolved the Americans badly needed Brest as a supply port. Rallying all German units in the area around FJR 2 and FJR 7, *Generalmajor* Ramcke's forces fought desperately for several weeks until the port fell on 20th September.

Taken into captivity the erstwhile ship's apprentice and now paratroop general underwent the lengthy and strenuous interrogations of the Allied War Crimes Commission but he was not convicted. General Middleton, who commanded United States 8th Corps in Brittany, said: 'I think he conducted the war in the tradition of a good soldier.'

RINGEL Julius *Generalleutnant*

Knight's Cross with Oak Leaves

Julius Ringel was born on 16th November 1889 in the town of Völkermarkt in the Austrian province of Carinthia. On leaving school he received military training as a *Landwehr* cadet in Imperial service and went to the First World War as *Leutnant* Ringel of the 2nd Mountain Regiment.

In the inter-war years prior to the *Anschluss*, Ringel served on the general staff at Innsbruck and as a battalion commander at Graz. The outbreak of war in 1939 saw Ringel however as an officer in the Wehrmacht. Service as Chief of Operations with the 3rd Mountain Division in Norway in 1940 was followed by his appointment as Commander of 5th Mountain Division. *Generalmajor* Ringel trained his new division for the assault on Greece, and in 1941 his troops broke through the Metaxas Line with Twelfth Army with great success.

Whilst still in northern Greece Ringel's men were summoned from Twelfth Army to partner 7th Air Division in the airborne corps for Operation 'Mercury'. After a strenuous march to an assembly point near Athens, the 5th Mountain Division spent three weeks training for the seaborne landing at Herakleion. In the event the division was air-landed in the west. The intervention of the 85th and 100th Mountain Regiments at Máleme late on the second day of the Battle of Crete brought decisive relief to the paratroopers. After the initial phase Ringel assumed local command of German forces on Crete.

After Crete *Generalleutnant* Ringel saw service with his division on the shores of Lake Ladoga in the Leningrad battle zone. In early 1944 the mountain troops found themselves fighting alongside the paratroopers once again in the mountains south of Rome at Monte Cassino.

Known affectionately by his men as 'Papa Julius', the *Generalleutnant* attributed his decorations to the devotion of his soldiers and his promotions to his advancing years. But an incident on a snow-covered runway on the edge of Lake Ladoga when a muleteer failed to acknowledge his divisional commander was too much for even 'Papa Julius' to bear. Displaying his Knight's Cross he asked his fellow Austrian if he knew what the symbol represented. Summoning a little interest, the soldier replied: 'Are you perhaps the new padre?'

SCHULZ Karl-Lothar *Generalmajor*

Knight's Cross with Oak Leaves and Swords

Karl-Lothar Schulz was born on 30th April 1907 at Königsberg in East Prussia and died on 26th September 1972 near Wiesbaden.

After gaining his school-leaving certificate, Schulz volunteered for the new *Reichswehr* and joined 1st Artillery Regiment as a recruit at Königsberg. Transferred to the Prussian Security Police, he was assigned in 1933 to the Special Purposes Police-group Wecke. Göring reorganised this special unit as a new State Police Group, which later developed into the Hermann Göring

Armoured and Parachute Armoured Divisions.

Schulz however was one of Bräuer's first officers in FJR 1 in the summer of 1938. Characteristically he persuaded his engineer company to go over with him from his former regiment. Assured by his men that they would do anything he did, Schulz declared: 'Then from today you are all parachutists.'

As a battalion commander *Major* Schulz was immensely popular with his men. He dropped with FJR 1 at Rotterdam and took part in the Battle of Crete. After Crete *Oberst* Bräuer made notes in his diary after a visit to a German theatre, which was packed with paratroopers. 'Neither I nor the actors on the stage knew what the sudden outburst of applause was for until I turned and saw that the commander of my 3rd Battalion had enter. the theatre. The applause was for "Lothar" returning to his men after a severe wound.'

Schulz progressed through the grades in 1st Parachute Divison and saw action at Leningrad and Orel on the Russian front; returning with the 'Green Devils' to the Mediterranean threatre. He was in the thick of the fight at Monte Cassino during March-May 1944 and later in the spirited defence of Bologna. *Generalmajor* Schulz commanded the division when it surrendered to Allied forces in northern Italy in 1945.

BRAUER Bruno *Generalmajor*

Iron Cross (2nd Class)

Bruno Bräuer was born on 4th February 1893 in Berlin. He served in the First World War as a non-commissioned officer. Seriously wounded young Bräuer returned home with the Iron Cross (2nd Class).

Bräuer joined the security police when first set up in Prussia, and later belonged to Prussian guard police as a section-leader. After the Hitler takeover on 30th January 1933, a special police unit was formed from men who were especially reliable. Bräuer commanded the 1st Company of this unit (*ZbV Wecke*) and went on to become a battalion commander of the Hermann Göring State Police-Group.

Bräuer joined the parachutists right at the very beginning. He was on the first Immans training squad course at Stendal, and was appointed Commander of the 1st Battalion of FJR 1. When the original airborne division was formed in July 1938, *Oberst* Bräuer was regimental commander of FJR 1.

In May 1940 FJR 1 was dropped in the Rotterdam area. *Oberst* Bräuer went in with the 1st Battalion at Dordrecht; the other two battalions being sent into action at Moerdijk and in Rotterdam itself.

Oberst Bräuer's regimental group parachuted at Herakleion during the first phase of the Battle of Crete on the eastern zone. Heavy losses were sustained until the paratroopers were relieved by Ringel's 5th Mountain Division. After Crete FJR 1 was transferred to Russia where the regiment was first located on the Newa.

Fate led Bruno Bräuer back to Crete after his first tour on the Russian front. As fortress commander he made many friends amongst the island population; but considerable partisan activity worsened the relationship of the German forces with their island captives. When in Germany *Oberst* Bräuer made persistent efforts to obtain better rations for his soldiers so that the strain would be relieved on the island's own resources. The colonel went into disfavour and was put on the reserve.

Generalmajor Bräuer was recalled to command 9th Parachute Division when it was formed in December 1944 for the defence of Berlin and Breslau. The division first went into action when the Russians stood on the Oder and was practically annihilated. The general was convicted as a prisoner for complicity in war crimes which are not explained. Already a broken man Bruno Bräuer was taken to Athens at the end of the war and shot by a Greek firing squad.

HEILMANN Ludwig *Generalmajor*

Knight's Cross with Oak Leaves and Swords

Ludwig Heilmann was born in August 1903 in Würzburg in West Germany and died in October 1959. He joined the army at eighteen years of age and served the twelve-year period of regular enlistment in the *Reichswehr*. In 1934 he was commissioned in Hitler's new German army.

'King' Ludwig, as he was popularly known, commanded a company of the 21st Infantry Regiment in Poland and afterwards in France. The exploits of the new parachute arm in 1940 aroused his interest and he soon volunteered for airborne forces. After parachute training Heilmann was posted to FJR 3 and took over the 3rd Battalion. The Battle of Crete saw the battalion in the bitter engagements at Galatas and Daratso, where so many German lives were lost.

In Russia *Major* Heilmann's 3rd Battalion of FJR 3 is unforgettably associated with the Vyborgskaya bridgehead. On 10th July 1943 the 1st Parachute Division was on its way to Sicily. FJR 3 now under the command of *Oberstleutnant* Heilmann arrived with the division in Rome and was shortly dropping on the Catania coastal plain. Both Allied and German parachute forces landed almost simultaneously in the same battle zone. The battles for the bridges at Simeto, Marcelliono and Malati all enhanced Heilmann's reputation as a commander. FJR 3 was one of the last units to leave Sicily.

FJR 3 fought tenaciously at Ortona on the Italian east coast until it fell to numerically superior forces at the end of December 1943. Heilmann's regiment won immortal fame at Monte Cassino. The three principal battles at Cassino have gone down in military history as reminders of the courage and human suffering of both the German and opposing Allied armies. FJR 3 evacuated its mountain strongpoint on the night of 17th May 1944.

The 5th Parachute Division, which was virtually destroyed in the Falaise pocket after the Allied landings in Normandy, was reformed in Germany and Holland under Ludwig Heilmann. His new division comprised mainly of former Luftwaffe ground personnel. Thrown into the Ardennes offensive at the end of 1944, *Generalmajor* Heilmann was awarded the Knight's Cross with Oak Leaves and Swords for his part in the battle. Captured by the Americans, he was sent to an English POW camp and released in 1947. 'King' Ludwig was greatly mourned by his former soldiers when he died in 1959.

GERICKE Walter *Generalmajor*

Knight's Cross with Oak Leaves

Walter Gericke was born on 23rd December 1907. Like so many of his future fellow parachutists, Gericke started out in life as a police cadet.

As a member of the State Police-Group 'GG', he volunteered as one of the very first paratroopers. As *Oberleutnant* he was made Commander of the 4th Company of the 1st Battalion of FJR 1 at Stendal.

In April 1940 his company was dropped at the Vordingborg bridge, which links Zeeland with Falster in Denmark. In Holland Gericke's 4th Company dropped at Dordrecht, but unlike Vordingborg the bridge objective was not taken intact.

In Crete the following year he landed with the 4th Battalion of the Air-Landing Assault Regiment at Máleme. His Battle Group Gericke fought with great distinction; and the award of the Knight's Cross was earned in recognition of his leadership and the determination of his men.

As Commander of 1st Battalion of FJR 1, *Major* Gericke next saw action under 7th Air Division in Russia. The battalion suffered heavy losses around

Stalino (now Donetsk) in the Southern Ukraine and also at Wolchow on the northern sector of the Russian front.

When Ramcke raised the 2nd Parachute Division in Brittany in the spring of 1943, *Major* Gericke commanded the 2nd Battalion of FJR 6. In July 1943 the division flew from Istres in the south of France to the Practica di Mare airfield near Rome.

As part of the Student takeover plan, Gericke's battalion was assigned to the raid on the Italian High Command at Monte Rotondo. The operation was successful although the Chief-of-Staff, General Roatta, had vacated his post.

The 2nd Parachute Division was transferred with Battalion Gericke in October-November 1943 to Russia (Zhitomir) where FJR 6 was practically eliminated. The 2nd and 3rd Companies of FJR 6 remained however in Italy at Perugia as a cadre from which Heinz Trettner's 4th Parachute Division was raised.

Gericke took over FJR 11 as regimental commander. The three regiments of Trettner's division each contained a special service battalion and these were soon assembled as Battle Group Gericke and thrown in at the Anzio-Nettuno beachhead.

Generalmajor Gericke was appointed to the command of the new 11th Parachute Division in January 1945 but this never amounted to more than a substantial battle group. After vigorously contesting the Allied Rhine crossings the division fell back into North West Germany and surrendered in the Oldenburg area to British troops in April 1945.

SCHACHT Gerhard *Generalmajor*

Gerhard Schacht was born on 6th April 1916 in the Steglitz quarter of Berlin. After taking his school certificate Schacht began to study law, but on 1st November 1936 joined a motorised reconnaissance section of the Wehrmacht. He was then attracted to the air force and was accepted by the Luftwaffe Demonstration Squadron at Greifswald.

But 'Owl, as he was known by his friends, did not stay long at Greifswald. Hearing of Bräuer's battalion at Stendal, Schacht volunteered for parachute training school. Bruno Bräuer posted Schacht to the 'Friedrichshafen Experimental Section', the codename for *Hauptmann* Koch's impending operation at Eban-Emael. During the successful landing on the Belgian fortress on 10th May 1940, Schacht led the assault detachment that captured the Vroenhoven bridge. Wounded at Vroenhoven, he spent some time in hospital and was later posted as General Student's ordnance officer at XI Air Corps. After service in Africa Gerhard Schacht went back to school at the Luftwaffe War Academy.

In October 1943 he was again with XI Air Corps, this time as Operations officer on the staff of the corps. From the end of 1944 he commanded a parachute battle group in defensive battles in Pomerania and Brandenburg. His regiment perished as FJR 25 under 9th Parachute Division, the survivors of which surrendered to Soviet forces in May 1945. *Oberst* Schacht retired wounded on 16th May.

A clandestine British commando action on 17th January 1944 shortly before the Allied landings at Anzio resulted in heavy casualties for the sabotage group. Prisoners were ordered to be executed in accordance with the Führer's directive to shoot prisoners taken in the irregular rôle. Schacht countermanded the order in time to save a Lieutenant Hughes as he faced a firing squad.

After the war Gerhard Schacht joined the Federal forces on the formation of the *Bundeswehr*: he served as military attaché in Teheran; and finally obtained the active command of the 1st (Air-landing) Division at Bruchsal. *Generalmajor* Schacht died quite suddenly on 7th February 1972 after a short illness.

KROH Hans *Generalmajor*

Knight's Cross with Oak Leaves and Swords.

Hans Kroh, or 'Hanne' as he was known by his soldiers, was born in May 1906 in Berlin. After leaving school he trained as a paratrooper whilst in police service and his transfer from a state police-group to the staff of the parachute school at Stendal-Borstel gave him an opportunity to develop his ideas on parachuting techniques and special equipment.

In May 1940 Kroh was serving as Operations officer to General Trettner, who at that time was chief-of-staff to 7th Air Division. *Major* Kroh succeeded Herbert Noster, a well-known athlete, in command of the 1st Battalion of FJR 2 and jumped with his battalion at Corinth in 1941. *Oberst* Sturm's FJR 2 was heavily committed at Retimo in Group Centre during the Cretan battle and all three battalions suffered heavy losses. Kroh's group was placed in a seemingly hopeless position until relieved from the west by mountain troops.

1st Battalion, FJR 2, was assigned in 1942 to Ramcke's brigade in the desert. *Major* Kroh's battalion participated in the rearguard action and the successful escape of the paratroopers on the southern sector of Rommel's defensive positions at El Alamein and fell back with the Afrika Korps through Cyrenaica and Tripolitania.

When FJR 2 joined the new 2nd Parachute Division, in Brittany in the spring of 1943, *Oberst* Kroh took over as regimental commander. Thrown in against Badoglio government troops after the Italian capitulation, the fight for Rome brought swift success against the Italians. *Generalmajor* Ramcke's 2nd Parachute Division was transferred in September 1943 to Zhitomir on the Russian front. At Schepetovka, Kirovograd, Novgorodka and Tal'noye in the southern Ukraine, FJR 2 shared the punishment of the other paratroop regiments facing superior Russian odds.

In May 1944 the division returned to Germany and arrived in Normandy before the invasion. The bulk of FJR 2 met its end in Brest. In Brest 'Hanne' Kroh took over command of the 2nd Parachute Division when Ramcke became fortress commander. Kroh was captured by the Americans and taken as a prisoner to England. He was not released until 1947.

Kroh returned to the army when the airborne arm of the new *Bundeswehr* was formed in the mid 1950's, and he was quickly named as Commander of the 1st (Air-landing) Division at Bruchsal in West Germany. The former police sapper died as a retired general on 18th July 1967.

WITZIG Rudolf *Oberst*

Knight's Cross with Oak Leaves

Rudolf Witzig, who was born on 14th August 1916, was the demolitions officer who landed inside the Belgian fortress of Eban-Emael.

Witzig's party of fifty-five parachute engineers destroyed two 120 mm. cannon and nine 75 mm. guns by explosive charges. When the exits of the fortress were blown in the 700-strong Belgian garrison was trapped; but then so were the parachute engineers until reached by the German relief force the following morning. The demolitions were achieved as a result of using new explosive devices as well as of hard training conducted in the utmost secrecy at Hildesheim.

In November 1942 *Major* Witzig led the parachute engineer Corps battalion that was operational with *Oberst* Barenthin's regiment in Tunisia. The 2nd Company had already been in action at the desert end of the El Alamein line in the Qattara depression with the Ramcke brigade.

The 21st Parachute Engineer Regiment was formed under *Major* Witzig at Moulin in France in early 1943 and sent by rail to Russia. The battalion first

156

went into operation in the area of Kovno in Lithuania; but later occupied positions on the railway line near Vilna in Poland. In October 1944 the battalion was withdrawn to Mecklenburg for rehabilitation. *Oberst* Witzig took over FJR 18 under 6th Parachute Division in late 1944 and led the regiment in Northern France, Belgium, Holland and in the Rhineland until surrender at Zutphen in April 1945.

BECKER Karl-Heinz *Oberst*

Knight's Cross with Oak Leaves

Karl-Heinz Becker was born in 1914. The *Fallschirmjäger* were not short of good officers but 'Black Becker' was certainly one of the most distinguished of the paratroop officers.

Becker went with the army to Poland and saw action at Stawiszyn near Lódz. His paratroop career is first recorded as *Oberleutnant* to the 2nd Company of FJR 1: Becker became regimental adjutant to Bräuer and was later promoted to the command of 3rd Battalion FJR 1.

Major Becker dropped at Rotterdam and at Herakleion with Bräuer's regimental group on Crete. In Russia his battalion was engaged on the central sector and in January 1944 he was with his men in Italy at Nettuno during the Allied amphibious landings in the Anzio area. In June Becker was in Normandy as Commander of the new FJR 5 under Schimpf's 3rd Parachute Division. Overwhelmed in the Falaise pocket, *Oberst* Becker was amongst the officers who escaped with their decimated units before the Argentan – Falaise gap closed tight.

Kampfgruppe Becker now came into existence. His specially assigned battle group earned Becker a formidable reputation in First Parachute Army as well as in Allied circles. In Autumn 1944 *Life* magazine wrote: 'If Becker has only five soldiers left he attacks with three and, if he has to yield to superior force, falls back on his two reserves.' Leaflets dropped from American planes offered a reward of 5,000 dollars for the capture of Becker, dead or alive.

von der HEYDTE Freiherr Friedrich-August *Oberst*

Freiherr von der Heydte was born on 30th March 1907 in München, the son of a former army officer. After taking his school certificate in 1925, he enrolled for militia service in the *Reichswehr* and was released in the autumn of the following year as a reservist in the rank of *Fahnenjunker-Unteroffizier*. During the next ten years he studied philosophy and law at Berlin, München, Vienna, Graz and Innsbruck.

In August 1936 von der Heydte was returned to the active list as an officer of the Wehrmacht, and was assigned in the rank of *Oberleutnant* as commander of an armoured reconnaissance detachment at Herford. He took part in the invasion of France as ordnance officer to the 246th Infantry Division and was promoted to the rank of captain.

After the fall of France *Hauptmann* von der Heydte volunteered for parachute training and was later posted to FJR 3. In the attack on Crete he was employed as a company commander and dropped with his battalion in Group Centre near Galatas – Alikianoú. His men were the first to enter Canea. In Russia he was in action at Leningrad and Schlüsselburg and further south at Wyborgskaja on the Newa and at Petroschino.

Major von der Heydte's battalion was assigned as demonstration battalion for 1st Parachute Division. He was responsible for developing techniques of night jumping, landing in water and also in wooded areas. Practice jumps were made with the men carrying personal weapons and equipment. Experiments in the military application of free-fall parachuting were carried out and continued when FJR 3 moved to the south of France in March 1943.

Major von der Heydte commanded a battalion of Ramcke's brigade at El Alamein in October 1942 and formed a rearguard action as the Afrika Korps retreated after the battle. He joined Ramcke as chief of operations in Brittany when 2nd Parachute Division was formed in early 1943. After the Italian capitulation during the Sicily invasion in the summer, the 2nd was allocated with the 1st to Rome, where von der Heydte saw action against Italian troops in the struggle to gain control in the Italian capital.

FJR 6 was refitted at Wahn near Cologne in January 1944 and posted to Brittany under the command of *Oberst* Freiherr von der Heydte. Thrown against the Normandy bridgehead in June 1944, his regiment earned the nickname 'Lion of Carentan'. Suffering heavy losses the regiment was formed up with First Parachute Army in the autumn in a defensive position on the Albert Canal. He commanded the reinforced battalion that made the valedictory demonstration by German airborne forces at Malmédy during the Ardennes offensive the following spring. Although badly wounded in the arm prior to the Malmédy operation von der Heydte jumped into action using a Russian parachute with a triangular canopy. This was recognised as one of the most stable parachutes in operational use.

Freiherr von der Heydte is the author of *Daedalus Returned*, which was published in the United Kingdom by Hutchinson in 1958.

SCHIRMER Gerhard *Oberstleutnant*
Knight's Cross with Oak Leaves

Gerhard Schirmer was born in January 1913 at Chemnitz near Leipzig in East Germany. After obtaining his school certificate he went to a police school nearby at Meissen.

Like many of his contemporaries he was attracted to the newly formed Luftwaffe and trained as a pilot in 1935 at Schleissheim near Münich. *Oberleutnant* Schirmer joined an Air Training Regiment and was quickly made a squadron-leader.

In May 1939 the airman volunteered for a parachute course. After receiving his paratrooper's wings, he was posted as a company commander in FJR 2 to Poland and saw action with the 5th and 6th Companies on the Wista in the area of Deblin. After the short Polish campaign he returned with the 2nd Battalion to Tangermünde near Stendal. FJR 2 emplaned at Tangermunde for the invasion of Fortress Holland and Schirmer's company engaged a battalion of the 4th Dutch Infantry Regiment at Katwijk airfield north of Rotterdam.

Both the 1st and 2nd Battalions were in action at the Corinth bridge on 26th April 1941, where after dismantling British charges the bridge was blown up by a shell. No one knows to this day if the hit was made by accident or design. He dropped the following month with his company at Herakleion on Crete. 2nd Battalion was amongst the units posted to Russia after the Battle of Crete and *Hauptmann* Schirmer saw action on the Mius river in the southern Ukraine.

In November 1942 Schirmer flew with *Oberstleutnant* Koch's FJR 5 from Athens into Tunis and was amongst the last men to return to Germany before the German surrender in Tunisia. *Major* Schirmer now accompanied FJR 5 as Commander of the 2nd Battalion to Zhitomir and Kirovograd in the Ukraine. Promoted *Oberstleutnant*, Schirmer was involved with raising FJR 16 in Germany and he flew as regimental commander into the Vilna fortress with four full battalions. FJR 16 (East) was heavily engaged on the Russian front at Kauen, Wilkowischen and Tilsit (Kirov).

At the time of the plot to assassinate Hitler, Schirmer was arrested by the Gestapo because of a connexion with the Count Stauffenberg family. He was released and fought with 10th Parachute Division along the Danube in the closing months of the war in 1945. After spending eleven years as a prisoner in a Russian work camp at Workuta, Schirmer joined the *Bundeswehr* in 1956.

KOCH Walter *Oberstleutnant*

Knight's Cross of the Iron Cross

Walter Koch was born on 10th September 1910, and died as a result of a motor accident on an autobahn in Germany in October 1943.

After leaving school Koch went as a police candidate at Bonn: he was transferred to the Prussian Security Police and was appointed lieutenant in January 1935. As *Oberleutnant* in the Hermann Göring Regiment, Koch volunteered for the paratroopers. Promoted to captain in April 1938, he was made Commander of the 5th Company of Bruno Bräuer's FJR 1.

In the autumn of 1939 'Experimental Section Friedrichshafen', codename for 'Storm Group Koch', was set up at Hildesheim. The training for the Eban-Emael operation was carried out in the utmost secrecy at Hildesheim. Four assault sections were formed under *Hauptmann* Koch's overall command: Steel (Altmann); Concrete (Schacht); Iron (Schächter) and Granite (Witzig). The targets for each section were the bridges at Veldwezelt, Vroenhoven, Canne and the fortress of Eban-Emael.

Major Koch, who was decorated with the Knight's Cross for Eban-Emael, led the 1st Battalion of the Assault Regiment in Crete and Russia.Finally *Oberstleutnant* Koch commanded FJR 5 in Tunisia in 1943.

Walter Koch was a tough soldier and a legend in his time. His methods as a leader did not always meet with the approval of his men; but when he thought he was right, he fought with ruthless determination and great personal courage.

DEUTSCH Heinz *Leutnant*

Heinz Deutsch, who was born in 1921, was not a senior officer but just a typical junior officer of the *Fallschirm Armee*. He joined airborne forces as a young artillery officer in January 1944.

At that time training for the Corps artillery brigades was carried out at Burg, Altengrabow and Schweinfust. The volunteers to handle the assault guns were all parachute volunteers from Flak and flying units although some were already trained paratroopers. The two artillery brigades that existed in 1944 were named the 11th and 12th Brigades.

The 12th Brigade was raised at Fontainebleau and transferred on the day of the Normandy invasion to the area south of St Lô. On 13th July 1944 *Leutnant* Deutsch shot up his first Sherman tank in this area. He himself was badly wounded but fought with his brigade again on the Nijmegen – Arnhem sector in the following autumn. From February 1945 Deutsch was with the artillery assigned to 7th Parachute Division until surrender near Oldenburg three months later. Hard battles were fought on the Lower Rhine and as the Germans strongly contested the Rhine-crossings.

On 24th February British tanks and infantry put in a particularly heavy attack on the town of Wesel. Deutsch's battery destroyed one Sherman and one Cromwell tank. The attack was abandoned and not renewed until 2nd March. The British then put in a night attack and reached the first houses in Wesel. Assault batteries Deutsch and Markert effectively provided the counter-attack supported by a platoon of paratroopers. Two Churchill tanks were knocked out.

Between 24th February and 24th May Deutsch's battery destroyed thirty-nine tanks of the Sherman, Cromwell, Churchill and Dreadnought varieties as well as four armoured scout cars. *Leutnant* Deutsch's record during this period was an example of the highest standards maintained by the paratroopers even in adversity.

SCHAFER Heinrich *Oberfeldwebel*

Knight's Cross of the Iron Cross
Iron Cross (1st and 2nd Classes)

Heinrich Schäfer was born on 27th May 1914 in a small village on the Neckar river. Schäfer first worked as a skilled barge skipper on inland waterways. He enlisted for short-term service in the army in 1936 and was released two years later as a non-commissioned officer.

At the beginning of the Polish campaign Schäfer was recalled and volunteered for the paratroopers. After Stendal he was posted to *Oberst* Meindl's Assault Regiment, and distinguished himself as a section commander at Máleme in the Cretan campaign. His personal courage in the face of the enemy lead to the award of both classes of the Iron Cross and promotion to the rank of *Feldwebel* (Company Sergeant-Major).

In Russia his reputation as an exemplary soldier grew. But Schäfer's greatest deeds were performed under *Oberstleutnant* Koch's FJR 5 in Tunisia. In February 1943 Axis forces had powerfully counter-attacked the United States 2nd Corps between Faid Pass and Gafsa and captured Kasserine and Sbeitla, but on 7th April the British Eighth Army advancing from the east had made contact with Eisenhower's Allied forces west of Tunis. The German and Italian troops were thus sealed off in the Tunis area.

Kampfgruppe Schäfer formed a battle group of fifty parachutists that held a nameless hill on the approaches to Bizerte from 28th April until 1st May. Known to the soldiers as 'Cactus Farm', the hill temporarily barred the passage of a superior Allied force; the advancing troops losing some 800 men dead and wounded and thirty-seven tanks. The survivors of 'Cactus Farm' were captured along with the remainder of FJR 5 near Tunis on 12th May 1943.

One day in August 1944 *Oberfeldwebel* Heinrich Schäfer stood amongst the lines of POWs on parade at Camp Harne in Texas. The camp commander, an American colonel, here presented Schäfer with the Knight's Cross he had earned in Tunisia.

355. 161